To MICK,
Best wishes and
thanks for buying all my books!
Cheers,

14 DEC 96

SUMMER THUNDER

Second Edition

by
Brian Shul

MACH 1, Inc.
Chico, California

MACH 1, Inc.
PO Box 7360, Chico, CA U.S.A. 95927

Images provided by American Design And Marketing, Inc.
Art Director: Lindy Hoppough
Set in 15/18 Adobe Garamond

Library of Congress Catalog Card Number: 93-078251

ISBN: 0–929823–13–3

First printing, December 1993

Printed in Singapore by Craft Print Pte, Ltd.

For all those Thunderbirds, past and present, who have given so much
of themselves, and inspired us along the way.

Acknowledgments

My sincere appreciation to the following individuals for their cooperation and assistance in the making of this book: Major General Thomas R. Griffith and Brigadier General Anthony J. Tolin of Nellis AFB; Capt. J.K. Switzer, Thunderbird narrator; SSgt. Linda Ipser, Thunderbird public affairs; Sgt. Jeff Wolfe, Thunderbird photographer; and Thunderbird alumna Sarah Johnson for mission essential data. A special mention of thanks for Thunderbird Commander/Leader Lt. Col. Daniel J. Darnell who was first to assist with the project and instrumental in its completion.

Foreword

Mach 1, Inc. is extremely proud to help commemorate the fortieth anniversary of the United States Air Force Thunderbirds with the printing of *Summer Thunder*. As the leading publisher of military works, Mach 1, Inc. has long excelled in representing the U.S. Armed Forces in a highly professional and informative manner. Maintaining the highest quality standards in publishing, our efforts have been rewarded with two golden Georgi Awards, laudatory recognition from the Secretary of Defense, senators and congressmen, and continuous praise from happy customers in America and throughout the world.

In keeping with this tradition of excellence, we were particularly pleased that the Air Force Thunderbirds, people who understand a great deal about excellence, entrusted their story to our care.

In author Brian Shul, we found the best man to tell that story. As an award-winning writer, accomplished photographer, and experienced fighter pilot, Brian brings an insight to this prestigious team that few would have. More importantly, he brings a passion to his writing, so that we all may share in the experience.

Mach 1, Inc. congratulates the Thunderbirds on forty years of achievement and is honored to commemorate their excellence with the publishing of *Summer Thunder*.

— Paul P. Farsai —
Publisher

Contents

Introduction

Most aviators who truly love airplanes can normally recall that distinctly impressionable moment in their lives when they were, in some fashion, first introduced to the winged machine; and how, henceforth all earthly endeavors seemed suddenly secondary to the stimulating thought of flying. For some, the moment approached quietly, the airplane perhaps resting elegantly on some airfield, silently luring the observer closer with seductive curves and shiny surfaces marvelously smooth to the touch. For others, the moment arrived sharply, with a blazing fury of speed and sound overhead, producing arcing trails in the sky that, while unfamiliar at first, were both terrifying and beautiful and could mesmerize the viewer into staring submissively at the spectacle for as long as it lasted.

I suppose first meetings have much to do with one's preferences or interests, and it was no different for me. I love military jet fighters. There is nothing else in the world like them. I probably feel this way since they were the first airplanes I ever saw up close. I was lucky; I was a kid during the '50s and '60s and was able to indulge myself in a veritable feast of Century Series jets flying in that era.

There was a time, though it is hard to remember, when I didn't care much about jets at all. I was about nine years old, and aside from some pictures and a few model airplanes, jets were just another item in a young boy's life, ranking somewhere behind bicycles, baseball cards, and Cub Scouts.

When my parents informed me I'd be going with them to a big air show one weekend, I was not too excited about the idea. I had other plans. My plans were overruled, and my fate was sealed, as my life was about to be changed forever. I was going to see the U.S. Air Force Thunderbirds for the first time.

As I stood staring at my first F-100 on the ramp at the show, I couldn't understand just what enabled this ungainly, albeit well-painted, airplane to hold my attention so securely. Then I saw the Team fly, and I understood.

There was sound like I had never heard before. That deep, powerful rumble that was signature to all the Century Series fighters. And the flame — no one had told me about afterburners, and how they bring the sound to increased levels of deafening and painful . . . ecstasy. But it was in the formation that I felt my life transformed. Putting those four planes together the way they did, so closely, was simply magnificent. I didn't know a thing about flying, much less formation flying, but I saw and felt such a togetherness in their flight that it changed the way I viewed flying, and life, forever.

Watching the Thunderbird F-100s dazzle us that day, I was experiencing my moment, from which there would be no return. The quiet seductress I had viewed resting motionless in the chocks was ungainly no longer and had transformed herself into a living, breathing entity of unbridled power, able now, to reach inside of me and take hold of my very being.

Mostly, my mind still recalls the simple beauty in the geometry of those planes together, flawlessly performing their diamond ballet in the sky, at angles that held us breathless. As four jets moved through the sky in unison, they became, in essence, one. Out of empty space, they had created something beyond the mere sum of its parts. When the solo jet turned that metal beast on its back and flew a straight line the length of the runway, my sense of danger was electrified, and I simultaneously felt both fear and wonder. Staring submissively, I was totally unaware of anything else. I did not understand the intricacies of all that I saw; I simply knew that I felt, somehow, every turn and roll with them and desired to experience what that incredible, terrifying closeness was like. As I watched that team perform, I could not compare my emotions to anything else I had experienced in my young life.

When the two solo jets joined the diamond to form the six-ship delta formation, my senses were full, as I had never witnessed anything so unbelievably precarious, and exquisite, all at the same time. As six red, white and blue jets rose gracefully into a deep sky that seemed to pull them upward, they roared past a cluster of small puffy clouds. As split rays of sunlight reflected across those silver finished wings, pulses of excited light danced across that formation and formed an unforgettable picture in a young boy's mind. With red-tipped noses seeking the vertical, dragging thick white plumes of smoke, the sight of that formation gripped me in a way that meant, though I didn't realize it then, the jets would have me forever.

There must have been others there that day who felt the same way, but none ran faster than I when the Team landed and the crowd was allowed to move forward to greet the pilots. I stared at the men in the neat-o suits, yet wasn't even sure why I was standing there. I saw people pushing and shoving to get an autograph. Autograph? I didn't want some handwriting on a brochure. I didn't even have a brochure. I wanted, well, to sit in the cockpit, and put my hand on the stick, and maybe go for a little flight later, and feel what these men felt; and mostly, I wanted to sit down one-on-one with this very impressive looking sky-god and ask him everything about how he did those, those *things* he did. Autograph? I was ready to offer them my *life*, and if they asked me to sign up for duty right then, I would have.

Figuring that they weren't quite ready for my services, I left the sea of people and walked around the wing to the back of one of the jets. You could do that in those days, though I am sure someone had said not to. I stood there, staring at that star-spangled tail, and couldn't resist reaching out and touching that perfect white star on the side of the fuselage, as if by doing so the jet would impart to me some of the mystical powers it surely must have possessed. I was hooked. I wanted to do this. A life had been altered.

Though they don't say they are in the life-altering business, the Thunderbirds will, every summer, alter lives across this country and around the world. They will do it in a most wonderful way, with the same kind of captivating aerial display I witnessed years ago, which spoke to me so eloquently of discipline, teamwork and excellence. They have been doing it for more than forty years now, with a pride and professionalism second to none, and always with that magnificent formation.

Many years after touching my first jet fighter, I was sitting in one, touching the stick and learning all about the unique world of formation that so impressed and mystified me as a young boy. I had found myself. The life altering process that had begun years before had finally manifested itself in a set of Air Force wings on my chest. Flying was all that I had imagined it to be, and more. Flying formation in jets was like nothing else I had ever experienced, and I loved it.

In the multi-mission, task-saturated world of a fighter pilot, formation is a tactical necessity, and it is performed on a daily basis. The leader–wingman relationship was one I became intimately familiar with, revelling in its structural concepts and striving to flawlessly perform its dictations. Penetrating weather together, joining up after a round at the gunnery range, entering the traffic pattern, landing on the wing, and even aerial refueling, all required the skills of close formation flying. Few things required as much attention or concentration — and practice. Flying on the wing could be miserably exhausting, but it could also be refreshingly beautiful, and I often experienced the joy which comes in creating that entity called "the formation" while flying in close concert with others.

The more I grew in my profession as a fighter pilot, the more I became aware of the level of difficulty involved with the kind of formation the Thunderbirds were flying as a matter of "routine." There was nothing routine about flying thirty-six inches from another aircraft, at 500 knots, pulling 4 G's.

Though many of us in fighter squadrons were impressed while watching the Thunderbirds perform, now with the trained eyes of professionals, squadron etiquette seemed to dictate that to publicly express such admiration for "a bunch of pampered guys in red flight suits who don't even carry the gun" was, well, uncool. But there we were, bringing our friends and families to the annual base air show and watching the Team as intensely, maybe more intensely, than our guests. And when the Team narrator's voice echoed across the public address system that instead of mere stunts, "the maneuvers you see today are performed by every Air Force fighter pilot as part of his tactical training," we would very nonchalantly acknowledge the admiration of our guests and pretend as if being inverted at seventy-five feet, perfectly level, was pretty routine. Meanwhile our palms grew sweaty and we stared in silent awe as ol' Number 4, in that big white Phantom, balanced on the edge of thrust available at the top of that loop, buffeting, but never losing position, at those dangerously slow airspeeds.

We were good, and yes, we did perform those types of maneuvers many times over in the course of flying fighters. But still, this was a higher level of expertise we were witnessing, one we knew was born of committed desire and continued refining of one's skills.

Over the years I learned and saw much in flying which impressed me. Delivering ordnance in propeller-driven fighters, performing air show demonstrations in the A-10, and flying the SR-71 over three times the speed of sound afforded me a variety of experiences. Throughout it all, however, I never ceased to be impressed with Thunderbird performances I frequently observed. As I watched many other demonstration teams, all exciting shows, I saw few as professional and none as precise. Each time I witnessed the beauty of that magnificent Thunderbird formation I was mesmerized with the joy of watching rarefied formation skills flown with such unwavering poise. To attain such a level of proficiency is never easy, and I knew that few people in the crowd could really appreciate the subtle differences in precision and difficulty that separates the Thunderbirds from other teams. I also realized there was much preparation behind the scenes by this team that the air show crowd would never see.

I have long wanted to do this book, but I had to wait for many things to fall into place. In the Team's fortieth year, I received my chance, and proceeded to write, so that others may come to appreciate even more than they already do, the Thunderbird experience. I wanted to write about the part of this team that is seldom seen, away from the air show performances: the demanding process of building a routine of excellence.

I spent a month observing and flying with the Team. I was already familiar with much of their operation, but came away with a renewed appreciation and respect for all that is required to produce that demonstration. I saw no glamor, no overbearing egos, no pampering. I did see real people, working so hard that they had little time to speak with me, or even notice me, which was just the way I wanted it.

This is not a history of the Team, but rather a celebration of all they do and how they do it. This book is not about individual team members, but rather the story of the essence of a team. To represent that essence, and all those Thunderbirds past and present, I chose the fortieth Anniversary Team. I could not have made a better choice, as the members of this particular team collectively represented all I had always felt was wondrously magnificent about the entire Thunderbird experience. No one staged any special performances during my observations. Everything I saw was just the way it is done every day, the Thunderbird way.

Ladies and gentlemen, low, and to your right, as you have never seen them before, the United States Air Force . . . *THUNDERBIRDS*.

All things excellent are as difficult as they are rare.

— B. SPINOZA —

CHAPTER 1

The Legacy

Study the ancient lore of North American Indian tribes, and you will find repeated references to an all-powerful bird of the sky. An omnipotent deity which caused thunder with the flap of its wings and, with flashing eyes, could hurl lightening toward earth. This legendary bird of thunder was said to control the forces of good over evil and light over darkness. Ancient drawings from many different tribes depict the bird in the red, white and blue colors typical of southwestern Indian culture.

On June 1, 1953, the United States Air Force commissioned its new aerial demonstration squadron at Luke AFB, Arizona, an area rich with Indian history. The official name selected for the Team was, appropriately, *Thunderbirds*.

That first Thunderbird squadron consisted of seven officers, fifteen enlisted men, and six F-84G Thunderjets. Today, the squadron is based at Nellis AFB, Nevada, and is composed of eleven officers, one hundred thirty enlisted men and women, and eleven F-16Cs. In 1953, the F-84G boasted a 5,600 pound thrust engine and there were no solo aircraft in the show. Forty years later, the Thunderbirds ride on 25,000 pounds of thrust in the mighty F-16, and two solo aircraft scorch the sky with powerful sounds worthy of the Team's namesake.

From its humble beginnings, the Team has grown and so too has the admiration from millions of people around the world. In 1956 the Thunderbirds transitioned to the F-100 Super Sabre, becoming the world's first supersonic aerial demonstration team. The match would last for thirteen show seasons, an era that many recall fondly as "the real air show days," before budgetary constraints, fuel shortages, tightening of FAA restrictions, and noise abatement procedures. The "Hun" was the last of the metal finish paint schemes and left its image fixed permanently in the memories of those who witnessed that shiny formation.

When the massive F-4E Phantom II donned Thunderbird colors in 1969, the memory of the single engined "Hun" seemed less impressive. The mighty sound of eight 'burners during the diamond takeoff still stands as the loudest and most impressive of show openers. This era of performances was all too quickly followed by perhaps the quietest of demonstrations when the venerable T-38 joined the Thunderbird family during a time of fuel shortages nationwide. Entering the high-tech world of digital flight controls, the Thunderbirds have flown the F-16 since 1983, returning to the tradition of performing in front-line fighter aircraft.

While aircraft technology has changed greatly since 1953, the Thunderbirds have maintained a consistency in formation and performance that reflects the great pride they take in their tradition of excellence. The basic show routine today still greatly resembles that of the early teams.

Formation is formation, regardless of the aircraft being flown. Though the speeds may change, the concepts remain the same. Flying close formation is the great equalizer amongst aviators and can humble a pilot in the blink of an eye. It is also a deadly serious game requiring the utmost in concentration and flying skills. Though it is called a "show," the Thunderbird performance is not to be mistaken for something simply fun, accomplished through rote memorization. It is a demonstration of skills reached through much training and practice. No one flies this way naturally, and the proficiency required must be sought tenaciously. Not every pilot wants to fly this kind of formation. Very few ever have.

In over forty years of performances, Thunderbird demonstration pilots number only 127. It is a select group. What they possess in greater quantities than others, is not the skill to fly this close, but the desire to want to learn how.

To fly alone is an inherently dangerous endeavor; to fly four airplanes this close together is to willingly trespass across normal boundaries of safety and risk. Dedicating themselves to continued long hours of concentrated practice sessions, Thunderbird pilots ably trespass where few can go. There is little, and sometimes, no, room for error.

In the painfully delicate world of balancing fighter jets in close proximity, malfunctions of either man or material are unforgiving, and the cost of any error can be catastrophic. Sometimes men have died in this business. They have not died because they were careless, or unproficient, or because they lost their concentration; they were simply engaged in the dangerous game of flying jets, where without warning fate can change the rules in a heartbeat.

In 1961, a two-seat F-100 was chasing the Thunderbird formation to help critique and check out the new leader. Completing a loop, the new leader witnessed a fireball on the desert floor below and realized the chase plane had hit the ground, killing both crew members. Piloting the chase aircraft was the highly experienced, previous Thunderbird leader. In 1966, in a relatively simple arrowhead loop, Numbers 2, 3, and 4 bumped jets. The result was two ejections, one jet damaged, and two jets lost. It happens. In 1967, during a performance, solo pilot Tony McPeak pulled his F-100D up for vertical rolls as part of the bomburst maneuver. His left wing ripped off from the fuselage in the pull-up. Remarkably, Captain McPeak was able to eject and sustained only minor injuries. Today he serves as the Air Force Chief of Staff and wears four stars.

Two Thunderbird pilots have lost their lives during actual air show performances, the low number a credit to a team that has flown 3,225 demonstrations in forty years. But the air shows themselves constitute only a small portion of Thunderbird flying, and while flying en route between shows, and during many hours of dedicated practice flights, sixteen others who wore the famous red helmet met their end.

The risk is accepted by all who strap themselves tightly into the white jets, but that is little consolation to the squadron when the gods of risk ask for payment in full.

No one could have predicted the difficulties the Team would endure during the T-38 era. The T-38 is a relatively simple aircraft to fly and is quickly mastered by experienced pilots. But there is no mastering chance and fate. In May of 1981, Thunderbird Number 6 lost control of his T-38 during a show, stayed with the plane and was killed when it impacted the ground. In September of that same year, the Team Leader's jet ingested a flock of birds while taking off from a show site, causing dual engine flameout. The commander was able to eject but was killed when the man/seat separation failed at low altitude. It was a heavy blow to the squadron, but the Team regrouped and by the end of the year had put together a new team for the following show season. In January of 1982, while practicing a routine loop near Nellis AFB, Lead's aircraft suffered a flight control malfunction and he was unable to complete the pullout from the back side of the maneuver. All four T-38s hit the ground with their pilots still at the controls. In an eight-month period, the Team had lost two commanders, and a total of six pilots. For the one team which, above all, prided itself on its professional approach to safe air show demonstrations, this was an unspeakably cruel blow.

There were some who called for the discontinuation of the Team altogether, calling it an unnecessary risk and expense. Others fought to save the one squadron which they knew represented annually the very best of the Air Force to the greatest number of people. There would always be risk, and fortunately, there were knowledgeable people who accepted that and knew that no other organization had gone further to ensure safety and proficiency in all that it did.

Pushing beyond their ill-fortune, the Thunderbirds steadfastly began to rebuild the Team, and a new plane, the F-16, was approved for the squadron. Like the Thunderbird of Indian lore, which could conquer darkness with light, the Team has continued and flourished, adding new show maneuvers to highlight the F-16's phenomenal capabilities.

Professionals who are in the business and understand the subtleties of formation flying agree that the Thunderbird performances today, while not as overly flamboyant as some teams, are the most impressive displays of precision formation flying in the world. There have been no Thunderbird fatalities since the transition to the F-16.

To fully appreciate this team is to understand that it is about people, and not just airplanes. Through the efforts of hardworking Team members, both inside the cockpit and out, Thunderbird jets have been able to thrill nearly 300 million spectators since that first fifteen-minute demonstration at Williams AFB, Arizona, in 1953. Each and every Team member wears the coveted Thunderbird patch with great pride, as they have earned it, and will continue earning it every day they are a part of the Team.

The air show routine which the public sees is only the final product of a myriad of efforts by many talented people. The extraordinary skills and Thunderbird precision witnessed by crowds of captivated air show spectators each year is not something that simply happens. It is sought and attained only after many hours of intense preparation. A prima ballerina may take years to perfect a dance routine. The Thunderbirds have less than four months each year to perfect their aerial ballet, before the show season begins. Unlike the ballerina who performs with the same legs each season, the Thunderbirds will introduce two to three new pilots to the formation each new season.

There is no more intense, and demanding, formation flying than occurs during Thunderbird training season between November and March each year. During this time the Team's skills, both in the air and on the ground, are developed to the point where the exceptional becomes simply routine.

This is not an easy process and there are no short cuts. It begins before the sun rises, before the pilots ever get to their jets, with the man who really "owns" the planes, the Line Chief.

A massive painting inside the squadron conference room depicts the different
aircraft flown by Thunderbird teams.

Home for the Air Force Thunderbirds today is Nellis AFB in Las Vegas, Nevada. Tours of the Thunderbird squadron are given twice weekly and make it the most visited unit on base.

Thunderbird hangar at night shows extremely clean work area. Even during the busiest work conditions, the squadron emblem on the floor is never stepped upon.

CHAPTER 2

On the Line

J et aircraft are incredibly complex machines. Without qualified maintainers, the planes would not get off the ground. In a typical year, Thunderbird jets will fly a total of 2,500 sorties and accumulate 3,300 flight hours while traveling 90,000 miles. With only eleven aircraft in the squadron, that adds up to around-the-clock maintenance.

The Team will perform fifty to seventy demonstrations each summer, priding themselves in continuing the tradition of never having to cancel a show due to maintenance. But it is not only the air show season which puts great demands on Thunderbird maintenance personnel. There is the winter training season when the Team will fly twice a day, five days a week, and sometimes more when necessary.

Planes 1 through 6 will normally fly every day, as they constitute the diamond formation and two solo aircraft. Numbers 7 and 8 are designated for the logistics officer and the narrator, and they will fly slightly less than the others during training season. That leaves three spare aircraft to replace birds that are down for repair, painting, modifications or periodic inspections.

Orchestrating the placement of people and planes on the flight line, is the job of line chief. He is normally a senior noncommissioned officer who has already spent a year with the Team. He has to please both the operations and maintenance sides of the house, while supervising close to one hundred people. He is responsible for seeing that all necessary maintenance has been accomplished and the jets are ready to fly.

THE LINE CHIEF

Basically, the aircraft belong to me, and I am responsible for everything that happens with them on the flight line. I start my people around two in the morning during training season. That way, we have time to hot cock the jets before they are flown that day. By performing engine runs on each jet, I feel we have a better opportunity to identify any potential problems on a particular plane before we try to turn it for two flights that day.

During this time I also ensure that the cockpits are set up properly for the pilots. This is important not only for the launch routine, but also from a safety standpoint. Each pilot has his own particular preferences concerning cockpit setup, and I feel it is important to make it as easy as possible for them by setting everything in such a way that they have to move a minimum of switches when they strap in. There is also the possibility of a switch being mis-set. I normally follow the crew chiefs around and double-check their cockpit setups. One time I found the auxiliary flap switch set incorrectly. That could have caused a serious problem for the pilot in flight if we had not caught it beforehand.

During a show, the line chief can be seen standing centered in front of all the jets as the crew chiefs assist their respective pilots with strap-in. From this position, he can cue off Thunderbird Lead and give silent signals to his men who, unable to see each other, will perform the launch sequence in unison. He is responsible for selecting and training the crew chiefs each season and coordinates the march-down routine performed at the start of each show.

 After a man has spent a year with the Team, he is eligible for selection as a crew chief. The other senior NCOs and myself evaluate his performance, and especially his attitude and motivation. You might think everyone's attitude and motivation would be extremely high all the time, but these guys are human and sometimes feel the stress during their first year on the Team. We start them out on night shift and make them work their way up to a better schedule the second year. Also, keep in mind that what we have here is a group of all-stars, so everyone usually thinks they have the best solution to every problem. I listen to all of them, and they really do have some good ideas, but then I tell them how we are going to do it and try to keep them focused as a team.

After about a year, they begin to understand the Thunderbird way of doing things, which basically means a Team member is going to become proficient in more than just his one area of expertise. They really come to understand the team concept here. Watch those crew chiefs in action when those jets land and you'll see people helping each other to get all *the jets ready for another go, not just their own.*

Every time the Thunderbirds land, whether after a practice or actual demonstration, the planes are immediately tended to. The ground crews will ensure that the jet is refueled, serviced with liquid oxygen and oil if necessary, and given a postflight inspection. Intakes are inspected, oil samples are analyzed, and the cockpits are set up for the next flight, including aligning the inertial navigation system. Then the jets are cleaned, from nose to tail every time. If the formation flew through rain, some retouching with paint might be needed on the leading edges of the wing and tail. If so, it is done on the spot by hand. Canopies are especially cleaned to ensure bug residue is not allowed to harden. If the Team is practicing a post-show parking alignment, then the jets will have to be pushed back into their normal start positions for the next go. This is most efficiently done by hand, and it takes about nine people to push an F-16 into perfect parking order. Anything left unfinished at the end of the day will simply be worked on into the night as necessary. The result will be a spotlessly ready jet for the next day's schedule.

The line chief directs the march-down and start routine from his position in front of all the jets. The crew chiefs will practice the routine daily during the training season, always under the constant eye of the line chief, who will evaluate their every move. When not launching or recovering jets, Thunderbird ground crews are most frequently seen cleaning them. It is no accident that the planes look as clean as they do.

Late hours are the norm here, and of course working on the weekends goes without saying. Basically it's a 365 days a year job. But I love the challenge. It keeps you on your toes. No days are ever the same here. I think we work better under the pressure, and actually come to enjoy it. When we go out on the road during show season, our hours are a little better, but then we give up having as many spare jets. If one breaks, we use number 7, the Logi's jet. We try to avoid using the number 8 two-seater for a show. I travel with the Team for every show. My being gone over two hundred days a year is a little hard on the family, but it's something they understand. I used to be fairly shy in dealing with people, but my experience on this team has cured me of that.

The best part for me is to see those planes take off, and the wheels come up; then I know I've done my job, and it's a great feeling. Of course I feel very fortunate to be surrounded by such capable people.

THE ENFORCER

One of the key people the line chief relies on to implement the job tasking, is the flight chief. While the line chief is responsible for the jets, the flight chief controls the people working on the aircraft. He assigns tasks and ensures that the right people are scheduled to work the problems. The flight chief is your basic no-nonsense sergeant. He is "the enforcer" in an arena where results speak loudest and there is often little room for discussion. He will kick butt when necessary and accept no lessening of the extremely high Thunderbird standards on the line. None. His people know this and perform. If they don't, they also know he will not hesitate to remove them from the flight line regardless of their sterling performances prior to coming to the Team. The flight chief also helps recommend people for the privilege of wearing the circular red-numbered patch that signifies crew chief status.

 I feel a little like the quarterback out there. I feel it is important to run things with a high degree of professionalism. You won't see anyone lacking in their effort here. If they are, they are gone. There is no room for anything but total commitment out on the line. Pilots' lives are in our hands when we work on that jet and we never forget that. People have to really want to be on this team to handle the schedule. I've seen some really terrific men and women out there doing a fantastic job and never complaining about the hours. I figure when someone volunteers for this job, they understand that there might be some eighteen-hour days, and those crew chiefs who wear the "red meatball" on their chest will probably work even longer. This Team is a great example of what can be accomplished when everyone in the group is working toward the same goal.

The hardest part of my job is blending all the different personalities together to work cohesively. I like all the different ideas they bring to the Team, but I also let them know that the mission comes first

Maintenance superintendent (l) confers with the flight chief (r) on the ramp. Lots of stripes, little nonsense.

Two crew chiefs per plane will maintain that coveted status for one show season.

Crew chief applies touch-up paint to her jet. Recent work on tail required the removal of rivets, taking the paint with them. When the required maintenance was completed, each and every rivet was re-touched with paint. No one directed this action, the crew chief simply did it. The official designation for the colors used on Thunderbird jets is " Thunderbird red," Thunderbird white" and "Thunderbird blue."

and try to keep them focused on that concept. Before coming to the Team, I managed airplanes; now I'm managing people and it's a challenge some days. I usually know when there is something wrong with the planes; it's harder to tell with people, and sometimes they might be having a bad day, and I have to stay on top of that situation. Airplanes are easier to handle.

During the training season, my day usually starts around 0230 so I can supervise the engine runs, and then I'll probably leave for home at 1700, unless there is some problem that needs my attention. I have a five-month-old little girl and haven't seen much of her since she was born.

When we go on the road, the challenge is to keep those jets flying for every show and that means spending hours in the hangar long after the air show crowd has departed. Many times I have never used the hotel room the Team provided for us.

But there are rewards too. We really can have a positive effect on the kids who see us and may be searching for some kind of role model in their young lives. One night we were working late on the planes and some visitors brought a young boy in a wheelchair into the hangar. It meant the world to that boy when we gave him one of our pins, and it's something we'll never forget.

NUMBER 11

The Thunderbird maintenance officer fills the number 11 spot on the Team roster. He works closely with the number 7 pilot (logistics officer) and his maintenance superintendent who, in turn, oversees the line chiefs. He is most often seen on the flight line with a portable radio in hand, coordinating actions necessary to keep things running smoothly.

One nice thing about my job is that you rarely have to tell people what they are supposed to do; they are usually already doing it. The people we hire are normally self-starters; they don't need much pushing at all. Sometimes the hardest thing is to just slow them down a bit. My guys, and gals, really take a pride in taking care of those jets. They baby those jets like they were their own. In fact, they take better care of them than they do most of their own things. People are normally amazed at just how clean the jets are, even up in the wheel wells. It's a daily process keeping the planes looking that good, but we wouldn't want to show the public anything less.

I've got a talented group of specialists working out there, and every year it seems like all of them apply for crew chief duty. Since the crew chiefs are in front of the crowd at every show, that is, of course, a great incentive for applying. I know a lot of people are watching the Team's every move during the course of a show season, and we really evaluate each member carefully for crew chief duty. That is probably the most difficult decision I have to make each year, and I listen carefully to my line sergeants' inputs before signing any approvals.

Line crew pushes a jet back to the starting position for the next launch. With everyone helping, the jets are able to be moved faster than if they were towed.

Close view of the tail shows detail of smoke generator. Oil is simply dumped into jet exhaust causing smoke which evaporates quickly. A separate oil system has been installed where the aircraft's cannon was housed.

Crew chiefs adorn the inside of the aircraft comm panels with a variety of names. Long a squadron tradition, solo Number 5 carries his number inverted in recognition of his inverted pass during the show. Crew chief for Number 3 formerly crewed the SR-71, thus the name, HABU III.

We put a lot of wear and tear on the jets during the training season, and we'll occasionally rotate the solo jets to other positions to reduce the amount of high G stress those airframes receive during solo maneuvers. We can easily renumber the planes with the changing of decals on the fuselage.

Once out on the road, my job becomes more challenging, as I really have to plan ahead several shows to ensure we can meet all our logistical needs. Remember too, we are flying into many non-military fields, and the support facilities may be less than adequate, so we may have to improvise. We take quite a large travelling kit with us on the C-141 during show season but invariably something will happen which will require some quick requisitioning. In case needed, the Team has two backup F-16 engines pre-positioned on the east and west coasts respectively. If necessary, I can commandeer just about any part we may need for our jets while at an F-16 base. The F-16 is a relatively easy jet to maintain, but we are flying them hard in the show routine and have to constantly watch for trends that can hurt us down the road. For example, the amount of inverted flight and negative G loading the solo jets get usually causes some leakage in the batteries of those aircraft, so we are constantly replacing them. We were also having a problem with the VHF radio antenna on the tail of the number 4 aircraft. Number 4 was flying so close to lead's exhaust in the slot, that he was melting the antenna.

If our country went to war tomorrow and needed these jets, we can make each plane combat ready within seventy-two hours. Basically the main modification necessary would be to reinstall the gun. Of course the jets would have to be repainted too, and that's what would take the longest amount of time.

Crew chief positions are eagerly sought by enlisted members of the team. Only the top performers are chosen, a tough choice amongst so many qualified people. Here, the Number 5 crew, identified by their "red meatball" patches (inverted, of course), prepare to ready the jet for the next launch.

The maintenance officer and his crew of supervisors, while responsible for maintaining the jets, must also maintain the delicate balance of keeping their people working harmoniously. Interestingly, the squadron functions as well as it does, because it puts a premium on treating its members with a high degree of dignity and respect. The supervisors are tough, but they listen to their people, and the resulting mutual respect is evident on the line.

TEAM SUPPORT

Keeping the Thunderbird jets ready to fly is a continuing process. Beyond the people seen busily tending the planes on the line are the many specialists who go unseen, but play as important a part in supporting the mission.

Home to these specialists is the distinctive white hangar at the north end of the Nellis flight line. The immaculately clean Thunderbird hangar is assaulted daily with the roaring reverberations of jets launching from the two runways at Nellis. No one complains, as this is the way one would expect it to be. On each side of the Thunderbird hangar are the offices and shops which run a variety of squadron functions.

On the flight line side of the hangar is the life-support shop which houses all the flying equipment such as helmets, oxygen masks, G suits and parachute harnesses. (In the F-16, the actual parachute is housed in the aircraft's ejection seat.)

Technicians prepare the pilots' flying equipment daily and ensure that it is pre-positioned in the appropriate jets prior to the aircrews ever getting to the flight line. The technicians are highly

Life support technician skillfully rebuilds oxygen mask of a "guest flyer" with the squadron.

skilled and may be required to make on-the-spot adjustments or repairs to any of the equipment. Simple things like a sticking exhalation valve in an oxygen mask, or a helmet with a defective radio cord, can potentially threaten the mission and are corrected immediately. Prior to joining the Team, Thunderbird life-support specialists have frequently been recipients of "Best in the Air Force" awards for their specialty.

Inside the main part of the Thunderbird hangar, a common sight is at least one plane on jacks, with numerous panels removed, receiving some required periodic inspection. The technicians working carefully around, and in, each section of the plane seem far removed from the glamour of standing beside a pristine aircraft before an air show crowd. But their work is essential and accomplished with the same exacting precision the public witnesses when Thunderbird crew chiefs march smartly toward the jets during a show start. Every time they fly, the pilots will entrust their lives to each actuator, line, connector, wire, nut and bolt of each plane. The technicians, working meticulously through every part of the complexity that is an F-16, understand this, and ensure it is a trust not broken.

The air show business is one of committed schedules and obligations to perform. Sometimes "maintenance required" bumps against the desired "operational ready" date, and scheduling decisions have to be made. The Thunderbirds are not simply in "the air show business": they are military professionals demonstrating their capabilities and their people to the public. As such, they make no concessions to rushing or foregoing maintenance they deem necessary to ensure the reliability and safety of their demonstration or their people. If there are schedules to change, it will be those of Team members who will stay a little later, or a lot later, to ensure the job is done right, the first time, on time. That the Team has never missed a scheduled demonstration due to maintenance speaks volumes of the squadron's professional abilities and integrity.

Enlisted maintenance personnel will stay with the Team for two years with an option for a third. The long hours and extended time away from loved ones not withstanding, most elect to remain Thunderbirds for a third year.

When one observes the highly skilled support crews at work and witnesses the obvious cooperation and enthusiasm, it is easy to imagine that their transition from regular Air Force specialists to Thunderbirds was as easy as sewing on the patch. Not quite.

Each new enlisted member selected to the Team must prove themselves during a twenty-one-day observation period. During this time, besides accomplishing their newly assigned duties, they will make time to diligently study the squadron's history. They will be held responsible for an in-depth knowledge and understanding of the Team, both past and present. It is a time of trial, both physically and emotionally, and will separate early, those who are unsure of their desire to be Thunderbirds. The "new guys" can be seen performing some of the less glorious tasks in the

A specialist carefully lubricates the actuators to the leading edge flaps. Periodically, the jets will receive this type of total overhaul. Stripped down, the F-16 exemplifies the complexity of the newer generation of fighters. Once reassembled, it is simply a work of art. In either condition, note that the Thunderbird hangar floor remains immaculate. Throughout the squadron, this sort of attention to detail is most common.

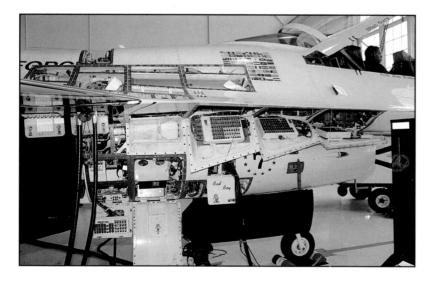

squadron, such as mopping the white hangar floor or polishing the brass. All are easily identifiable by the absence of the large Thunderbird patch above their breast pocket.

Even though there is a certain amount of good-natured kidding, the process of earning one's patch rises above the sophomoric hazing traditions of other organizations. Here it serves as an integral step in preparing new Thunderbirds for the personal flexibility, effort and commitment to the mission which will be required of them as Team members. Becoming familiar with the squadron's history well prepares them later to answer the public's questions about the Team at any number of non-air show functions where they will represent their Air Force.

For enlisted Team members, the process of becoming a Thunderbird culminates with the "patching ceremony," a squadron tradition closed to public viewing. It is here, on the shiny floor of the hangar, before other squadron members, that a new teammate receives his or her Thunderbird patch. This is accomplished amidst much good humored cajoling from the Team. As the patchless member stands at attention, Thunderbird Lead fires off difficult questions concerning the Team's past. The new member, surrounded by a circle of grinning and gesticulating Thunderbirds, must ignore all interference, and concentrate on the commander's questions. Nerves are tested. Some have impressed the squadron with their ability to answer the most obscure of questions. Others have fought their own private battle against shaking knees and slight lapses of memory. But all who wear the patch have endured, and once that coveted white emblem is firmly placed on the new member's shirt by Thunderbird 1, it is not easily removed. To ensure the new member feels secure, the first sergeant kindly staples the patch to the member's shirt on the spot, and all squadron members then shake hands with, and sincerely welcome, the Team's newest member. Inside the unique world of fighter squadrons is the unwritten protocol that says, we only kid the hardest, the ones we respect and like the most. There is no greater face of pride than that of a newly "patched" Thunderbird.

For Thunderbird pilots, there is no patching ceremony: there is the training season and the building of a formation. In that demanding process, the pilots too, will learn that their patch must be earned. Everything everyone in the squadron is working toward is embodied in the formation. The long hours of maintenance, the engine runs, the cockpit setups, are all done so that six airworthy jets can take to the sky and enable the pilots to perform that demonstration. Performing the aerial demonstration safely, and professionally, is the squadron's mission, and it is taken seriously. No one takes it more seriously than the pilots themselves, for they will be the most visible representatives of that mission.

When a new Thunderbird pilot crosses the threshold of that white hangar for the first time, he leaves the world of normal squadron flying behind and begins a journey toward proficiency that is as challenging as anything he will ever do. Like all pursuits of excellence, the desired skill level is only attained after many hours of practice. For Thunderbird pilots, the arduous road toward demonstration pilot begins over a barren stretch of sagebrush and sand in the Nevada desert.

The squadron museum is rich with history and tradition. New Thunderbirds will become intimately familiar with the squadron's history before they can earn their patch. Here, a new member endures his "patching" ceremony as the commander contemplates the score of that last answer.

During training season, preparing the jets to fly begins before sunrise.

CHAPTER 3

The Springs

Nestled in the foothills forty miles northwest of Nellis AFB, rests a small community called Indian Springs. There are no Indians, and whatever springs once flowed have long since dried up. The single high school, few modest homes and two gas stations would easily go unnoticed were it not for the large Air Force runway sitting adjacent to the lone highway accessing the area. For nine months out of the year it is a quiet town, existing in the isolated silence between Death Valley and the oasis of Las Vegas.

Every winter, though, the calm that is Indian Springs, is penetrated by the sound of jets overhead. Very close, overhead. As certain as the return of swallows, each winter season Thunderbirds descend upon the Indian Springs airfield to commence the start of another training season.

The men who come to fly this formation are already accomplished fighter pilots. They are experienced professionals who have repeatedly proven their mettle in their former squadrons. They volunteered and were selected for the Team, not only because of their accomplished flying skills, but because they had a burning desire to learn to fly in this intricately difficult manner. And it is that desire which will most sustain them through the humbling process of reaching for, and attaining, a new plateau of skills. Often they will be beaten by a formation that seemingly takes pleasure in its disdain for the skills of its members. But it is not the nature of these men to accept defeat, in any form; rather, they are more prone to persevere. And they do until, in time, the skills required seem less forbidden, and the formation becomes their own. And while it is never conquered, in its expression, the formation embodies all that these men strive to represent.

Practice begins modestly with two-ship formations which introduce the new Team members to what "Thunderbird close" really means. Twice a day, practice flights are launched from nearby Nellis AFB. These continue for three months. The demands on the ears of local residents are slight when compared to the physical stress endured by each Thunderbird pilot, daily, throughout the training season.

Relatively few people in the world have piloted a jet airplane. Fewer still have flown jets in formation. Since a very select few will ever experience the art of Thunderbird flying firsthand, a better understanding of the difficulty of its precision may be gained by relating it to a more familiar earthly concept.

Imagine someone gives you a brand new sports car, a Corvette perhaps, and says you can drive down a cleared road at 130 miles per hour and not worry about getting any tickets. Then when you get comfortable with that, there is another guy, in the same kind of car, who is going to lead you down the road. In order to stay together, you must drive your car so that you keep your front tire aligned with his door handle, all the time, no matter how much the speed varies, and you mustn't stray out laterally any farther than the width of one bucket seat. Don't worry about looking forward to see where you are going anymore, the lead car will take care of that; you just concentrate on those position references, no matter how uncomfortable that may seem. This is so much "fun," we are going to add two more Corvettes to this group, one on the opposite side of the leader, mirroring your position, and one directly behind the lead car, so as to create a geometrically pleasing diamond shape to the group. Of course this means you will be a little closer to the edge of your side of the road now, so you'd best stay right in your designated position. Besides, if you start feeling too uncomfortable, just look — no, just think — about the fourth car in the rear, who is so close to the leader at 130 miles per hour that he is counting totally on lead's ability to maintain a very consistent foot on the gas pedal.

When everyone's proficiency has grown with practice, the leader will forego the straight and level path and take you over some steeply hilled roads, complete with hairpin turns. This will require variations in your speed of between 30 and 130 miles per hour, so be ready to make rapid accelerator and steering adjustments to maintain your position. To help you, the leader will verbally cue these changes over your radio, so listen up. Oh yes, I forgot to mention that every time

Thunderbird practices begin with two-ship formations. These will be some of the most demanding sessions for the pilots, as they will be introduced to "Thunderbird close" in arm-draining flights lasting twice as long as an air show performance.

The two solos return to Nellis from a training flight; one of the few times regular formation spacing is flown.

you go into a turn, your body will effectively weigh four to five times its normal weight, so steering and keeping your eyes on your references could be a strain. Also, to give everyone a more "positive" feel during the rapid, small corrections they'll be making throughout a wide range of speeds, all power steering has been removed and your vehicle will require the steering strength similar for a large truck. Now, don't run off the road and don't bump into anyone else, and yes, those two cars following you are going to join the group eventually, for an impressive six cars driving as one.

Difficult, you say? Imagine then, doing it at 600 miles per hour through the air, inverted and rolling, and pointing straight down at the ground, and in a hundred ways you could only dream of in your car. The formation would be so impressive that people would come from far and wide to witness the spectacle. And they do, by the millions each year, to see the Thunderbirds perform their aerial artistry. And often, one's car seems less potent a machine on the drive home from the show.

Though the car analogy may help in our understanding of the Thunderbird formation, it must remain earthbound and can only give us a hint of the dynamics and demands involved in such precision flying.

Flying formation, good formation, is a study in concentration and trust. As the leader pulls the formation upward into a vertical climb at the start of a loop, several things occur which take us far from the car analogy. First, the onset of gravitational forces will feel like someone has tied lead weights to your arms. With constant movements required on the stick and throttle to maintain position, this G force can affect your ability to make the fine corrections necessary to maintain the reference on Lead. And speaking of references, Lead's airplane is now the only "horizon" you have, as you will see only a backdrop of blue sky as his nose comes up and you continue to stare toward his aircraft. Eventually, you will notice the horizon moving through Lead's jet as you start down from the top of the loop. If the horizon is obscured by weather, you will feel very spatially disoriented. Regardless, you must ignore the temptation to respond to those things you see peripherally, such as the ground rushing up at you. Even when you are a thousand feet above the ground, peripherally you can feel like impact is imminent. Concentration. Besides the basic hand-eye coordination necessary to fly the formation, you must concentrate to overcome the physical forces, the disorientation induced by lack of normal level reference, and the mental forces of fear or doubt. When a fighter pilot talks about "gutting it out on the wing," he is referring to the intense concentration required to combat the many disruptive forces playing on his mind and body while in formation.

Putting three airplanes close to the leader at the same time adds another dimension of distraction. While you are busy making all those corrections to maintain your position, so are the other guys. Quite unannounced, someone may make a sudden movement which can distract you, stop your heart, or kill you. Hopefully the wingmen are good enough to rarely cause such movement. Hopefully, Lead never does, since it will affect everyone simultaneously. Trust.

Every Thunderbird formation is a model of structure and order. The aerial display which captivates the wonder of young and old alike, is not choreographed purely for spectator entertainment. Instead, it is a carefully selected array of maneuvers designed to showcase the professional skills of the Air Force fighter pilot. The flight maneuvers flown at each show represent a selective blend of basic aerobatics and advanced combat tactics, all presented with the professional élan which has become the Thunderbird trademark. Team members, all volunteers from the tactical flying force, are themselves representative of the training and basic abilities of all Air Force pilots. Through the precision of the formation, they seek to demonstrate the ultimate expression of those skills publicly at each show.

Each pilot has one position to fly and will occupy only that position. Each position in the formation is unique and requires different specific skills and, once learned, a pilot's position is not interchangeable.

Each position in the formation is designated by number, starting with the leader, who is Number 1. In keeping with the Air Force standard, the Number 2 position is on Lead's left. Flying off the leader's right wing is Number 3. To form the renowned diamond formation, the Number 4 aircraft is positioned directly behind and slightly below Number 1, in the slot. The two solo

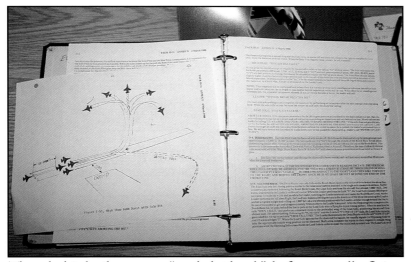

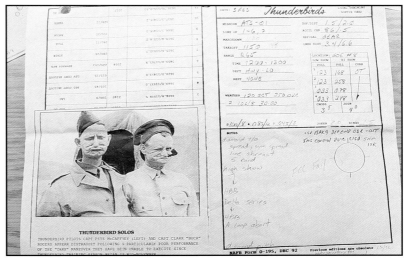

THUNDERBIRD SOLOS
THUNDERBIRD PILOTS CAPT. PETE McCAFFREY (LEFT) AND CAPT. CLARK "BUCK" ROGERS APPEAR DISTRAUGHT FOLLOWING A PARTICULARLY POOR PERFORMANCE OF THE "OARS" MANEUVER THEY HAVE BEEN UNABLE TO EXECUTE SINCE

Thunderbird pilots must "read the book" before actually flying the maneuvers. There are numerous manuals which require thorough understanding and, due to the pace of the flying schedule, winter weekends are normally filled with study.

As navigation officer, Number 4 fills out the day's line-up card for the formation. In this case, some "diamond humor" directed toward the solos was copied to everyone's card.

For every flight, there will be a post-flight inspection. Here, crew chief ensures all switches in cockpit are set properly.

demonstration aircraft fill Numbers 5 and 6. When the solos join the diamond formation, they will join to the outer wings of Numbers 2 and 3 to form the larger delta formation.

Throughout the various maneuvers flown, the alignment of the aircraft will change to create different formations, but each pilot always retains his basic position number, even when his relative position changes. For each position of each formation flown, there are very specific guidelines and precepts governing the movements, position references and responsibilities of each pilot. These guidelines are detailed within squadron formation manuals which serve as the starting point for all maneuvers.

Until one has done it, few realize the intensity of control inputs by each pilot while in close formation. Watching the elegant lines of the Thunderbird formation moving smoothly through the sky, the observer on the ground is easily led to believe that all is calm and steady within the cockpits. Some have even been heard to suggest that the jets' autopilots can maintain proper formation position and the pilots need only monitor cockpit instruments. This is as false as thinking symphony music is produced in an orchestra by the movement of the conductor's baton. Like the musician who positions fingers in a complexity of rapid movements across an instrument, creating the proper notes, the formation pilot deftly moves hands, fingers and feet continuously in the cockpit to maintain his aircraft in that one proper position which, in turn, helps orchestrate the solidarity of the formation as a whole.

In theory, maintaining position in a regular formation of jets is a simple process of control inputs. To maintain fore and aft position, the left hand judiciously regulates the throttle for more or less power. To control vertical placement, the right hand pushes or pulls (ever so minutely) on the stick, resulting in upward or downward movement. Lateral spacing can be controlled with left or right movements on the stick, or more subtly, by pushing on the left or right rudder pedals with either foot.

Orchestrating these movements at 450 knots, a couple of feet from another airplane, requires a great deal of finesse and is incredibly exhausting even after a few minutes. Because any deviations in position are amplified by the closeness of each aircraft, each pilot's attention is strictly focused on Lead's aircraft for position reference points. Given the impossible task of trying to duplicate perfectly Lead's flight path, pilots in the formation are continuously making small corrections. There is no perfect formation, only the aggressive, continuous corrective inputs which can make it look perfect, when done with expertise. This is a process which begins with taxiing out to the runway and ends only after the jets are shut down in their parking spots after a thirty-minute performance.

In the midst of making continuous control inputs, which in time become second nature, the pilots will also be pressing radio buttons, opening and closing the speed brakes, and activating the show smoke on and off, at various times during their aerial routine; all requiring the deft

Early morning takeoffs are the norm during training season. Here, the solos take off from Nellis en route to the Springs. Note Thunderbird hangar in background.

On a bleak winter afternoon, Number 5 holds his favorite position and tries to please his toughest audience — the "Logi" below.

A wake-up call for the folks at Indian Springs, as the team "closes it up" for the beginning of another practice. Seen here from the Number 2 jet, the deeper stacking of the Delta formation is evident. In the diamond, Number 4 would be farther forward. Note the missile rails of Numbers 2 and 3 in Number 4's view.

movement of fingers across throttle switches. Meanwhile, throughout it all, there is the constant strain of the changing G forces sustained in the vertical and tight turning maneuvers.

Straight and level flight is performed at 1 G, the same as a person experiences standing on the ground. When the aircraft's flight path is rapidly changed (climbing or turning) the basic laws of physics require an opposite and equal force to the new vector. This results in the G force which acts on the aircraft and, of course, the person sitting in the aircraft. It is very similar to the centrifugal force experienced on rapidly spinning carnival rides. The force felt at 500 miles per hour, however, is a bit more of a "crunch" on the body than the 30 miles per hour carnival ride. The faster the speed, the greater rate of movement that can be attained. Speed alone does not create G forces, it simply acts as potential energy for "G available." So an aircraft travelling at 450 knots, pulling up aggressively into the vertical, may experience 4.5 G's in the pull, for example. Once pointed straight up, however, if that upward vector is maintained, the relative G force is back to normal, or 1 G. Most young children are aware of this concept the first time they put a rock into a sling and swing it over their head. The force which is pushing the rock into the sling is the same type of force pushing a pilot's body into his seat during changes in his vector relative to the earth. A normal show routine will see the jets come back with G meters usually registering -1 G to +6 G.

All of this would make flying air show formation difficult enough, but there is one more factor which contributes heavily to the pilots' work load in Thunderbird cockpits. It has to do with the positioning of the flight control trim switch. The trim switch is a small button on the stick which enables the pilot to electrically reposition the control surfaces with a simple movement of his thumb. This reduces the pilot's work load, relieving arm strength to hold stick pressures for various flight conditions. If trimmed properly, an aircraft will remain in a desired attitude (normally level) when the pilot's hand is removed from the stick.

Each Thunderbird pilot, while on the wing, incredibly, flies the entire show with full nose-down trim. In this condition, if the stick were let go at any time, the jet would rapidly pitch nose down. In order to keep it from doing so, a constant pull of near twenty pounds of pressure is required, all the time, throughout each maneuver.

This uncomfortable forward stick pressure is induced for a purpose. As the formation approaches the top of a loop, the airspeed has decreased to less than 200 knots, and the lead aircraft will be pulling close to only 1 G as it enters what is called "the float" over the top. If the jets were trimmed normally, as the formation arced across the top of the loop, the wingmen would find themselves transitioning in and out of the zero or negative G range, correcting to stay in position. This would necessitate some pushing and pulling on the stick with radically changing G conditions, a dangerous situation in close formation. With full nose down trim, there is always a "heavy" stick, and as the formation enters the "float" over the top of the vertical maneuvers, each pilot can simply reduce the back-stick pressure, instead of having to push forward as the formation nears zero G. Having this positive G "feel" on the stick enables the pilots to stay in position with more stability at the low end of the speed/G envelope.

There is a price to pay for this compensation, however, at the high end of the speed/G spectrum. The back-stick pressure required to pull out of the loop is now added to the twenty pounds of pressure incurred with the nose-down trim. On top of the normal physical stress in this type of flying, the added stick pressure creates some very sore forearms at the end of the day.

This arm fatigue is most noticeable during early training season, when Thunderbird pilots are paced through two-ship practice. These sessions often last twice as long as the time required for an actual show performance. These initial workouts are extremely fatiguing for the pilots, but eventually with increased comfort levels in close formation, comes increased arm stamina.

With the exception of colorful jets trailing lines of white smoke overhead, there is little at Indian Springs in the winter which resembles an air show. There are no crowds, and no rows of aircraft parked neatly on the ground. Occasionally, a startled rabbit scurries across a taxiway as the solo jets pummel rows of tumbleweed with the sound of afterburners, and few, if any, people in the immediate area stop to watch the process of aerial refinement occurring twice each day.

There is one, however, who watches intently, every maneuver and every movement of each jet, and critiques and grades every "performance." That is his job. He is Thunderbird Number 7, the logistics officer. No practice, or show, will commence unless the Logi is in place to observe the flying. He is assisted by a small support crew who man the video cameras and operate the communications trailer. Coordinating with the tower, the Logi owns the airspace for the time the Team is overhead. He not only grades each session, but he acts as the air and ground safety observer. The Logi, in the number 7 jet, will sometimes fly in chase on the formation for more direct observation. He is in constant radio contact with Thunderbird Number 1 during every performance and can terminate a practice or show instantly if he sees something unsafe.

Armed with full video coverage of the Team in flight, the Logi can debrief the Team accurately on every maneuver. There are two certainties in life as a Thunderbird. There will be no demonstration flying without the observer, complete with radio and video capability on the ground, and there will always be a debriefing following each flight. Always. After every practice, and after every air show flown. No matter how late the hour, or how fatigued everyone is, or how well the Team has flown; every frame of video footage is reviewed every time — critically.

All personal feelings, egos, and past performances, are set aside when it is time to sit down and debrief the flight. Video coverage of the formation is shown in slow motion, stop action, or frame by frame as necessary, many times over. There is little that goes unnoticed. Steadfastly stringent in their standards, a Thunderbird debriefing will frequently be in its second hour before an "attaboy" or "good maneuver" comment is issued. There are no short cuts to getting it right.

To assist Number 7 with video coverage, Number 8, the Team narrator will often fly in a chase position with the formation and "shoot" the Team through the gunsight, recording the formation on his aircraft's internal camera system. He will begin his narration practice at the Springs when the Team is able to fly the full profile of show maneuvers.

The continued process of critiquing each performance brings the formation to new levels of proficiency, since "good enough" simply isn't, to this team. No one critiques the Team harsher than the Thunderbirds themselves, and it makes for a refinement of skills rarely witnessed today in other endeavors.

Though few may take notice each winter, eight proud men at the lonely edge of Indian Springs, will strive together in pursuit of a goal. Their quest will require much from inside themselves and, once completed, will enable them to reach many beyond themselves. From the individual trials and triumphs of each cockpit will be formed an entity far greater than any of its parts, a symbol of trust and accomplishment — a formation.

The Logi and crew observe another practice at the Springs. While aide behind Logi copies down his critique comments, radio specialist helps as safety observer, and cameraman videotapes every maneuver. This crew will drive daily to the Springs, returning home after the second practice flight is completed. One member will speed videotape back to Nellis in mid-morning for use in debriefing first flight.

An arrowhead formation pierces the desert silence moments prior to the pull-up for a loop.

CHAPTER 4

The Formation of a Team

The rarest gems on earth are formed only after the protracted processes of geological movements and pressures are completed. So too, each winter after many arm weary hours in two-ship practice, a special type of diamond is formed in the sky over Indian Springs. It is unpolished and will take more time to shine its brightest, but it marks a critical milestone in each new team's development.

From ground level, the Thunderbird formation is seen as one entity moving through space, each aircraft a stable corner of each point of the diamond. To see the formation from the cockpit of any of the three wingmen is to become acutely aware that it is a moving, breathing force, fluidly balanced on the razor-thin line separating the exquisite from the terrifying. By its very nature it is never the same any two times, and each pilot will have his own remarkably different perspective of the formation each time he flies.

Unnoticed by many who watch is the fact that the diamond always rolls left when performing a rolling maneuver. Not particularly noteworthy to the spectator, this fact means that Numbers 2 and 3, while separated by the thirty-one feet of Lead's airplane, are actually worlds apart in movements required to maintain their respective positions.

LEFT WING

The first time I was shown what my position looked like, up close, I wasn't really sure I could do it. Riding in the back seat of the number 8 jet, I was uncomfortable not being the one in control, especially being that close. Through a well-defined building block approach, though, you eventually become comfortable with your one position, and I suppose that's a credit to the Air Force method of training. It's very demanding mentally, in that you're always seeking the perfect position, and you're never quite there.

One of the hardest things to get used to was the discomfort of being rolled into all the time. Once I was able to fly my position with some degree of proficiency, the next challenge was flying it with the whole diamond. I remember the first time that Number 4 came into the slot, it felt like we were all too close and I kept feeling like I wanted to move out a bit, but slowly our comfort level increased. After that, there was learning all the techniques needed to make the formation look correct optically. Few people realize how many adjustments we make to our positions throughout the routine so the formation looks geometrically correct to the spectator on the ground.

Take a relatively simple maneuver like the diamond roll, for example. From the ground, it looks pretty tame, but there's a lot happening. When the Boss starts us up, as Number 2, I can't be behind in the pull at all. If I am, then I'll be pulling a little harder to compensate, and as the Boss rolls into me I'll be slightly high. You really don't want to be high when the formation is rolling into you. As soon as the left roll begins, I begin pushing on the stick while bleeding in a little right rudder. As we are rolling left, the right rudder input keeps my jet from looking wide in the formation. This cross controlling of left forward stick and right rudder is quite uncomfortable, especially at the rapid roll rates we use. As the formation goes inverted in the roll, I take out some of the rudder and then, as we complete the roll, I coordinate the movement of the stick back to normal with the release of the rudder. This has to be done at a rate that doesn't make my aircraft appear to be misaligned as we pass show center. So how do I know where show center is while I am staring at Lead's aircraft? That just comes with practice.

When we first started training, I wasn't aware of anything else except Lead's missile rail in my face. I was many times thankful that Lead cued the next maneuver on the radio as it was very easy to become totally detached from anything happening beyond the Boss's airplane. After a year, the situational awareness you can develop is uncanny. I now know exactly where we are in relation to the show line, and have even seen the solos and the crowd below us during the routine.

During the training season, my arm felt like it was going to fall off some days, but, like the other guys, I wasn't going to be the one to say "uncle." We simply got used to being exhausted at the end of the day. I used to think that going one-on-one against another F-16 back in my former squadron was a good day's work, but I never worked so hard in flying as when I came here.

When I got through my first training season, I thought I was doing well and felt pretty confident. After six months of air show flying, I saw just how much I had improved and realized maybe I wasn't all that good at the end of the training season. It's a process the new guys will all go through.

Once the show season starts, the Team will continue its practice demonstrations. The narrow tolerances between a successful show and disaster demand it. Formation skills are perishable, especially at this advanced level, and the Team does not go more than a few days without flying a show or a practice show. Flying the routine four times weekly is considered a minimum for the proficiency required, and will be accomplished for the duration of any Team member's two year tour. Only twice a year is there any time off for the pilots at all — several days in July during the mid-season break, and about ten days at Christmastime. During a typical show week, the Team may fly the show "only" four times, as compared to the ten times a week they were flying during training. To keep the fine edge required to perform at this level, the Team will be right back out at Indian Springs the day after returning home from a trip, for more practice.

The Thunderbirds could fly an easier routine, and it likely would continue to impress air show audiences everywhere. But as professionals, representing their entire service, they demand the best

The diamond position as seen from Number 2. In upper photo, the normal reference, as the formation is inverted over the top of a loop. Lead's airplane is the flight's sole attitude reference, and sky and earth must be ignored to maintain positions. Just keep that missile rail in your face! Lower photo shows Number 2's position during a pass-in-review maneuver, as he now slides in closer. The leader is actually in about a forty-five degree left banking turn here. When you can count the rivets, you're close.

from themselves and take a distinct pride in being able to fly the most difficult of maneuvers safely and expertly. Since no Team member finds this type of flying naturally comfortable at first, their formations are vivid testimonies to what one is capable of accomplishing through disciplined efforts.

Some maneuvers the Team flies are more difficult by the very nature of the formation required. Every member of the diamond agrees that the trail-to-diamond roll, is the most challenging maneuver to perform correctly. The maneuver starts with the jets in a single file line behind the leader (trail). As they start upward, they re-form to the diamond while completing a roll. For years this maneuver was flown from left to right in front of the crowd, and the intricacy of the movement from trail to diamond was lost to the spectator by the angle of view. Recently, the maneuver was changed to approach the crowd from behind. This brings to full view the dynamics of the jets moving into the diamond from trail.

Part of the difficulty of the maneuver stems from the Thunderbirds' insistence that a pure trail formation be flown; that is, the jets must be flown directly behind and slightly beneath each other in a straight line. Other teams fly a type of trail formation that has the wingmen offset slightly, making their position simply a deeper variation of their wing position. In pure trail, Numbers 2 and 3 are required to fly a position similar to what only Number 4 flies normally in the diamond. Stacked in descending order, Number 4 is now at the end of the line in trail and feels the amplification of the slightest movement the others which may cause a ripple through the formation. If Number 4 is thrown slightly out of position during the trail formation, it is often the result of some movement by Number 2, sitting under the Boss.

★ ★ ★
★ **2** ★   *As Number 2 the most challenging maneuver to fly correctly has to be the trail-to-diamond*
★   ★   *roll. When the formation is in trail, it is a simple follow the leader line, but there is nothing*
★ ★ ★   *simple about flying it properly. I am second in line, right beneath the Boss, so the slightest movement by me will ripple through the entire formation. As the line of four jets pulls up, we quickly transition back to our diamond positions. Number 3 and I try to make our moves look somewhat uniform, something we can only determine by viewing the video tapes. Moving left and forward, I have to then stop that momentum by correcting back right, but I can't correct too much since Lead is getting ready to roll left, into me. There's a lot of finesse in that maneuver — and some terror too.*

A maneuver I enjoy more is the pass-in-review, and I know we are off to the start of a good show when we fly a really tight one. It occurs early in the show and is the tightest formation we will fly all day. We all are adjusting our positions closer on that one, and I can look up and see Lead's missile rail eighteen inches above my head. Not a fun pass on a turbulent day.

Pure trail. Pure hell.

This year, Numbers 3 and 4 were new to the diamond, so there were some new adjustments to make. On takeoff, for example, if Number 3 is a little out of position, then I'll try to match him to make it look symmetrical. It's a challenge, because something different will happen every time we go out there.

During my first training season, I didn't want to kill myself; this year I don't want any of these guys killing me.

Most fighter squadrons have thirty to forty people to perform various duties necessary to keep a squadron running effectively. The Thunderbirds have eight pilots who share a variety of tasks to ensure all squadron requirements are met.

Number 2 serves as the operations officer and, as such, assists the leader when necessary. He will devise each day's flying schedule and keep the commander advised of any flying regulation changes. A daily routine of briefing-flying-debriefing, and then doing it again in the afternoon, leaves little spare time, and making out the schedule, grabbing a quick lunch, taking care of paper work, and briefing the commander on important events, usually all occur in the space of thirty minutes between flights. Thunderbird pilots simply can't afford to show up for work late, or stay home sick.

RIGHT WING

★ ★ ★
★ **3** ★   *From the ground, you really don't get a true perspective of how close this team flies. When I*
★ ★   *saw my position for the first time, I thought the guy flying me was sticking it in there extra*
★ ★ ★   *tight to impress me. Then I realized that it was the actual position that I would be flying.*
I was speechless.

Going through the two-ship phase of training, I was always amazed to see on the tapes the frenzied movement of the horizontal slab on my jet, indicative of my wrestling match with the stick to maintain position. The Boss used to joke that maintenance was going to have to replace the actuator in the tail of my plane.

Eventually we all got smoother, and one of the main reasons is that Lead is so consistent. Because we can depend on him to do things the same way each time, we can anticipate the required movements accurately. When he says, ". . . nose coming up . . . and rolling . . . ." we know that on the 'u' in up, he will start his pull, and on the 'r' in rolling, the aileron will be deflected on his aircraft, beginning the roll. It has to be that precise to keep everyone moving in unison.

As Number 3, I am always being rolled away from. Throughout the dynamics of a diamond roll, I am continuously making corrections to my normal position to ensure it all looks right to the crowd. As the formation rolls away from me, I will be making a slightly larger arc through the sky than the other jets and compensate for this with slight rudder into the formation. Using aileron for these corrections

The difficult trail-to-diamond roll. Above, the Boss has called to re-form the diamond and the wingmen have started their move. Note the extensive use of rudders to move the aircraft without deflecting the ailerons. Below, Lead has started his roll, and Numbers 2 and 3 charge to regain their positions while aligning their noses with Lead. Number 4 will secure his slot position as the formation is inverted. The incredibly fast roll rates employed by the Thunderbirds requires total anticipation by the wingmen.

would create too much of a wing movement and destroy some of the solid look to the formation. It also would be a bad technique to use when the solos join up, because they would have a more difficult time maintaining good position on myself and Number 2 if our wings were continuously rocking. Once past the 90 degree point in the roll, my jet is out of view to the crowd and I can use more rudder as necessary. As we continue around to the 270 degree point, the jets are planform to the crowd, so it is important to have the noses aligned with Lead, so then I ease out some of the rudder and we should be pretty straight. To make these little moves, it's necessary to know exactly where you are in relation to the crowd throughout each maneuver. We probably use more rudder with this jet than anyone else in the F-16 community.

The dynamics of a Thunderbird performance, do not allow for the pilots to warm up to the flying routine. The intensity begins immediately with the takeoff, as Lead explodes off the runway in an impressive sixty degree climb attitude. There are no second chances to make it all look good. Rolling down the runway, the wingmen are all anticipating that pull. In order for Number 4 to make a clean move to his slot position after takeoff, it's critical that Number 3 maintain good position on Lead throughout the takeoff and departure. If he moves aft, or gets low, it can have serious consequences for Number 4, who is moving beneath him to get to the slot position. It is a maneuver that can only be practiced once on each flight and requires not only a great deal of anticipation and concentration, but also complete trust between 3 and 4.

Moving quickly from one maneuver to the next throughout the show, each pilot will see a variety of different positions besides his normal station in the diamond formation. Each presents new challenges to the ever-present goal of maintaining the proper position.

In the five card loop, for example, Number 3 finds himself having to fly a position quite unlike his normal formation. Like a playing card, the formation puts four airplanes in a box pattern with a plane forming each corner, and one set precisely in the middle. Instead of the normal three foot spacing used in the diamond, the planes are now nearly thirty feet apart from each other. While this may result in slightly less tension in the cockpit, it actually makes holding a precise position more difficult. Due to the nature of the desired geometric design in the five card loop, if any of the planes are not equally matched in spacing, it is more dramatically obvious to the observer. As always, the spacing starts off Lead, and it is Number 3 who sits in the front row of the formation setting the spacing the others must match.

★★★
★ **3** ★ *In the five-card loop, I am basically performing a line-abreast loop on Lead. The challenge is maintaining an even position with him while keeping the distance between us consistent throughout the loop. The two jets in the back row at least have a plane in the middle to reference off; I have to use three different references on the Boss's airplane while looking ninety degrees*

The beautiful five-card loop. Abeam the leader, Number 3 will set the spacing. Wedged between four other jets, Number 4 must maintain a steady position, with little room to maneuver.

off my left shoulder. For my vertical alignment I try to keep the canopy rails even on Lead's plane, and for fore and aft position I align the lip of the inlet on his jet. The tough one is lateral spacing. For this I try to maintain a position which aligns the wing light and the tail light on Lead's jet. The lights are about twenty-five feet apart, so it's not a real comfortable reference. Throughout the maneuver I have to keep checking all three references, or I won't know which one needs correcting when I see them start to move. If I move from the desired position in any axis, then all the references will look different. It's a fun maneuver. I like the challenge of having to be a solid cornerstone up front that the others will set their spacing by.

The Thunderbird diamond 360 maneuver is probably not near the top of the average spectator's list of "most impressive" when reviewing a show — but it should be. The maneuver consists of the diamond performing a 360 degree turn, at show center, at four G's. It closely follows the impressive maximum rate 360 degree turn in full afterburner by solo Number 6 — a tough act to follow. The diamond turn does not use burners, it is a wider turn, and it's not as loud as the solo's, so it is understandable that few might realize that, by its very makeup, it is a more difficult maneuver. In this case, what is invisible to the eye — the 4 G's — is what makes the diamond 360 so demanding, and a superlative example of the kind of muscle formation few would attempt to perform with such precision.

The 4 G's the diamond sustains when pulling up into vertical maneuvers quickly diminishes as the aircraft slow near the top of their arc. In the diamond 360, a level maneuver, there are a constant 4 G's sustained throughout the entire circle. It is an agonizingly long turn for the pilots who must pull against four times their normal weight while making the delicate corrections required to keep a tight diamond. Simply breathing can become a chore.

Not wanting to increase the G loading in the turn, the one thing the Team could do to make the maneuver even more uncomfortable to fly, would be to make it a right turn, instead of left. By the position of the pilot's right hand on the F-16 side-grip stick, greater strength can more easily be generated for a left turning motion, especially during high G turns. The Thunderbirds perform the 4 G diamond 360 to the right.

For Number 3, it is one of the few times the formation, though not rolling, does turn toward him.

3 *The diamond 360 was a tough one for me during training. The duration of the maneuver just plain hurt some days. Once in the turn, I am the closest to the ground, but I never get to see the ground, as I am staring at Lead, and that wasn't real comfortable at first, especially at the low altitude we're flying the maneuver. I know that if there's a problem, I really don't have anyplace to go, being sandwiched between the ground and the formation.*

Over the desolate Springs area, an arrowhead formation heads earthward. Good side view of horizontal tails shows deflections from neutral, indicating heavy pulling on the sticks.

During the training season, I could judge my comfort level with how tense my body would get during each maneuver. I knew I was getting comfortable with the diamond 360 when my neck stopped hurting. Now, the only one I still get tense for is the trail-to-diamond roll.

On that one, I'm back in that sandwich position, this time between Numbers 2 and 4 in trail. Then as we go to diamond, I not only have to move laterally, but forward on somebody rolling away from me (Lead). I'm glad we only do that once in each show.

THE SLOT

They call it the "slot" and many air show observers say it is the most difficult position on the Team to fly. The word *difficult*, is a very relative term on this team, so that would be hard to decide. Without a doubt, however, flying the Number 4 position is totally unique.

Flying on the wing, albeit not this close, is something Numbers 2 and 3 can at least relate to from their previous flying experience. Sitting in the slot, tucked tightly behind and beneath Lead, wedged between the missile rails of the wingmen, is quite unlike any normal formation position. While skimming the edge of Lead's jet exhaust, Number 4 has an unmatched, though precarious, view of the entire formation. With three jets sitting in his face, he has little room for escape if necessary. He can drastically alter the shape of the diamond by flying too close or too far aft on Lead, and he takes center stage at every show with the first dynamic move of the demonstration, when he first slides into the slot, moments after takeoff.

4 *My adrenaline starts the second we get on the runway, as I am already thinking about that takeoff move. At 150 knots the Boss rotates off the runway with a 1.8 G pull and sets the formation for about a sixty degrees nose high climb. Number 3 needs to hold good position, and then I can slide into the slot, hopefully with enough power differential to move forward. Lead tries to give me a little power, but sometimes, even in full 'burner, it's hard for me to keep up if his afterburner has shifted into a higher stage. There are five different stages of afterburner in this jet, and with all the "help" from the digital engine control, Lead can't always keep it precisely in that third or fourth stage.*

A simple thing like raising the landing gear on takeoff becomes an art form. The gear handle is on the left side of the cockpit. The motion of releasing the throttle and lifting the gear handle with your left arm would normally cause some movement to the ride side of your body. But you can't be making undesired inputs with your right hand on the stick, so you have to draw a line down the middle of your body and be able to move your left and right sides completely independent of each other. Moments after liftoff, your left hand will be snapping the gear lever up while your right hand continues to smoothly pull on the stick — much easier said than done.

The view of Lead as seen from the slot. If the Boss coughs, Number 4 will know it.

Twice a day, during the winter, we perform that takeoff before the world's toughest audience, our peers at Nellis. Even though we accept a learning curve, we want it to look good every time.

For the first six months, I never knew whether I was going to have a really good takeoff or not. In my second year, I didn't have that anxiety; I had control of it instead of it controlling me. Even with a great deal of F-16 experience, I felt like I was starting over when I began my first training season. I really wanted to fly the slot, and when I flew along with the former Number 4 and saw it all, I couldn't believe I really wanted to do this. That was definitely the most exciting flight of my career.

They put 4 under the Boss right from the start, and eventually I became comfortable in my little "spot." In setting my position on the Boss, it's more by feel really, not like the precise references the wingmen might use. Actually, getting closer to Lead sometimes makes my position easier to maintain. I have to watch burning the tail antenna though; maintenance doesn't like that too much.

Sometimes it's a bit disconcerting staring at Lead's tail, watching the chaotic movements of 2 and 3, and seeing the ground rush up at you all at the same time. The wingmen can see the Boss's head in the cockpit, and I think that is somewhat reassuring in that they can see his gesturing throughout the maneuver. All I see is three airplanes heading for the ground, sometimes, and it's impossible for me to accurately assess at that point if we are going to smack in or not. You learn to have an incredible amount of trust in your leader. You have to, in order to fly like this.

Like the wingmen, Number 4 has certain maneuvers that he finds more appealing than others, and like the rest of the diamond, he has a healthy respect for the trail-to-diamond roll. At the tail end of the trail formation, Number 4 feels the worst of any rippling through the formation.

★★★ ★4★ ★★★ *I went into the trail-to-diamond roll tense, for two years. It was never the same. Instead of being tucked under the familiar confines of Lead's jet, there were now two other jets between us. I believe I preferred flying under just Lead. It was more of a reaction maneuver and there was at least one "whoa" every second show.*

One time the general wanted to ride along in the slot during training season, so I flew him in the two-seater. During our ascent in trail formation, Number 3 eased up on his pull slightly, and we found ourselves staring into his 'burner can. That was definitely a "whoa" as we both pushed on the stick. The general was pretty good about it though, as he realized that was all part of flying this type of formation. After landing he said, sort of kidding, that flying with Number 4 was "too dangerous" and he'd stick to flying with the other guys. I never did control that maneuver, and the general never did fly with me again.

As Lead pulls the formation aggressively off the runway, left hands anticipate the quick move to raise the gear handle. Once the wheels are up, Number 4 moves trustingly through the shadow of Number 3 en route to the slot.

Number 4 also performs a maneuver each show which, while barely noticed by the crowd, requires a maximum effort of finesse and situational awareness. It occurs near the top of the line abreast loop. One solo jet joins the diamond to form a line of five jets abreast of each other. Pulling up into a loop, the five jets pull a beautiful plume of smoke into the vertical. At the top of the loop, the solo splits off from the other four, and it is this dramatic separation which most catches the crowd's attention. Meanwhile, the other four jets have continued across the top of the loop and then move to re-form into diamond formation. While line-abreast, Number 4 is on the left wing of Number 2 and, once the solo splits off, is at one end of the line. As the wingmen move aft on Lead, into their diamond positions, Number 4 must move aft, beneath Number 2 and into the slot. The movements here are compounded by the fact that initially, the formation is still in the "float," inverted, and by the time the diamond is re-formed, Lead will be back into a heavy pull on the back side of the loop. Though few may be noticing, Number 4 must delicately time and judge his movements to smoothly move into his slot position as the formation starts down.

★★★
★ **4** ★ *The first time I saw that maneuver, I thought it was simply dangerous. There is so much*
★   ★ *happening at once; it is very fluid. It requires an immediate shift from concentrating on the*
★★★ *line-abreast references, to moving aft, down, across, and then pulling to match Lead coming out of the "float." It is very easy to get deep and be out of position when the formation starts back down. It is somewhat disorienting, and if there is a cloud layer erasing the horizon, you are pretty much "floating" in your mind for a good portion of the show. I concentrate very hard during that maneuver.*

One of the most fun maneuvers is the crossover following the bomb burst. It is also one of the hardest to get just right and sometimes requires some plain luck to make it all work out. The idea is to get all four jets crossing at show center at the same time. Factor in the winds and it can be tricky. When I roll out after the bomb burst and am heading into show center, I have to pick up Number 1, and basically set myself nose-on to him. At 12,000 feet apart, head-on is a poor reference for closure rate though, and I try to pick up Number 3 on my left for a better timing reference. I also have to keep everybody in sight since I will be passing underneath everyone at the cross. We are crossing at about one thousand miles per hour closure rate, so there isn't much time to make corrections. If I see Number 3's smoke disappear, I know that he has gone to 'burner to make up spacing, and I will do the same. If we are too close, then you'll see speed brakes coming out, something that also will interrupt the path of smoke from the jets. Throughout it all, my basic contract is to miss the Boss, so I have to have him in sight. It's terrific when it all works.

Of course, immediately following the cross, we pull up into a vertical rejoin, and that's pretty sporty for Number 4. I'm basically rolling out above Lead and pointing my nose down to rejoin into the slot, at low altitude. Once I commit my nose straight down into the rejoin, there's no place else I can go, and

Seen from Number 2, the diamond banks sharply in their climb out, just moments
after taking off from Nellis.

I better have judged my closure, speed, and altitude accurately to avoid hitting Lead or the ground. I have pulled that little jet pretty hard more than once during that maneuver.

I know that we are trying to reach a level of precision here that most people won't be able to appreciate fully, but we have to continue to strive for perfection, or we might become complacent. We take great pride in the precision of our formation. I was having a little problem with my smoke for a while and that really bothered me. First of all, we try to get the smoke on and off in unison, and I mean exactly in unison. We've been known to go over the video film frame by frame to see whose smoke the Logi caught coming on a nanosecond too soon. My biggest problem was that after I had smoke on, I kept doing something with the rudder that was giving my smoke a deviation, making my flight path appear irregular. This was especially noticeable in the bomburst, after the diamond had split apart. I just couldn't correct it for the longest time. One day Lead told me to visualize that every time I had smoke on, there was a giant trail of cotton tied to my butt and my goal was to keep it straight. It's gotten better lately. The smoke may seem insignificant compared to the actual flying, but our approach to it is indicative of the attention to detail that permeates everything we do.

I've really come to enjoy flying in the slot, and would not trade my experiences on this team for anything. There is always a combination of excitement and joy during a show, but that can be wiped out instantly when something happens that jolts you back to the reality of danger which surrounds you. Though the second year is easier, I would never say that I could completely relax in the formation; but there does come a point where everyone feels like they are in perfect harmony with what everyone else is doing. It's truly graduate level formation flying.

I am currently lifting weights to build up my left arm so it matches my right.

Sometime near the completion of training season, the Thunderbirds will practice aerial refueling in preparation for the upcoming show season. Once on the road, aerial refuelings will occur frequently. Here, rendezvous is made with a KC-135 nearing the Grand Canyon. After receiving fuel, the formation will proceed to Indian Springs for another practice routine.

From the back seat of Number 8, the refueling boom comes uncomfortably close to the canopy prior to reaching the F-16's receptacle. From the tanker boom operator's view, Thunderbirds fly formation even when receiving gas.

Flying in concert with the Thunderbird diamond formation are two solo aircraft. Precisely coordinating their entries and exits to the show line, they form a sort of team within a team. Designated lead, and opposing solo, Numbers 5 and 6 bring an extended dimension of precision to the Thunderbird performance. In addition to their sequenced maneuvers, they will also join up with the diamond to form the six-ship delta formation near the end of each demonstration. For this formation, they are designated left and right solos and will keep that position for the two years they are on the Team. This continuity also holds for the various solo maneuvers flown. If the pilot flying the number 6 jet performed the inverted pass in his first year on the Team, he will continue flying that manuever in his second year, now as the lead solo, Number 5. This continuity is important in developing the skill and critical timing involved with the different solo maneuvers.

Watching the Thunderbirds perform, one might assume that to fly the solo positions would be easier and maybe even more fun than being a part of the diamond. Perhaps for some, it has been both, but the demands and skills required to fly either solo position are, like the diamond, not to be underestimated. In addition, there are the body bending paces which each solo puts his jet through. No one on the Team puts more G's on his body, both positive and negative, than do the solos in every show routine.

With every bit as much precision (and difficulty) required in learning to fly the diamond, the solos will learn to fly inverted at 75 feet, perfectly level; perform crisp eight-point rolls; forcefully hold a knife-edge pass when the aircraft wants to do anything but that; crunch through an 8 G max rate 360 degree turn in full afterburner; hit show center simultaneously while passing head-on to each other at 800 feet per second; and hold the jet on the edge of a stall for a 104 knot pass at an incredibly high pitch angle. While this is only a partial list of the solo's routine flown during each show, it is indicative of the type of performance/capability maneuvers primarily demonstrated by the solos. When it is time to take a "break" from such endeavors, the solos will join up with the diamond, flying on the outer wings to form the delta formation. To fly the show as a solo is to understand great contrasts in speed and maneuvering.

Overriding everything the solos do with their aircraft is precisely when and where they do it. The Thunderbirds take great pride in producing a performance that shows some aircraft in front of the crowd at least every thirty seconds. The solos are constantly working in coordination with the diamond's exits from show center, timing their entries safely to ensure minimum time between maneuvers. Far from being a separate portion of the show, the solos are integrally linked to the diamond in a well-orchestrated blend of radio calls, formations and timing.

Having two solo aircraft enables the Team to maximize the variety of formations and maneuvers flown for the crowd. Throughout different sequences, solos are seen individually, together, combined with the diamond, opposing each other, and in stark contrast to the diamond, as when one solo, miles from the runway, chases and overtakes the landing-configured diamond formation at show center.

What the crowd sees at show center is normally the culmination of a maneuver which began several miles from the field. At speeds ranging from 350 to 600 knots, the solos use prominent landmarks at specific points from each end of the runway to help with their alignment and timing. To assist in their accuracy, Thunderbird pilots are able to utilize helpful features of the sophisticated F-16, by reading extremely accurate data on cockpit heads-up displays. The HUD will show airspeeds, G loading, distance to go to a designated point, and the aircraft's attitude relative to the horizon, just to name a few.

No show is ever flown without Thunderbird Lead, and the solos, first making an observation flight around the show site. This is normally accomplished in a helicopter or light aircraft the day prior to a show. During this flight, hazardous obstructions are located which may not have appeared on maps, and key features offset from show center are pinpointed which will be used to assist in the timing of maneuvers during the demonstration. Prior to each demonstration, the Team is also issued detailed aerial photographs of the show site, and uses these to plot distances accurately.

The solo routines at every Thunderbird performance are normally crowd favorites, but few people realize the diversity of demands placed upon Numbers 5 and 6 during a show.

As a solo pilot, I have a very healthy respect for where the ground is. We want to show the capabilities of this jet in a professional manner, and even though it may look "reckless" out there to the observer, it is anything but that. Each maneuver is designed with a built-in safety factor and only stepped down to lower altitudes after total proficiency is demonstrated by the pilot. Of course that doesn't mean it doesn't get violent out there sometimes.

During strap-in, I cinch the straps very tight, not only on the lap belt, but on the survival kit connectors as well. It's not very comfortable at first, but five minutes into the flight you never even think about it. We don't carry any extra items in the cockpit and ensure the map case is empty prior to start. During training season, on the way to the Springs, 6 and I will roll inverted, and push some healthy negative G's. This will ensure that any loose items in the cockpit will float into view under the zero and negative G loads.

As lead solo, I am responsible for the timing in the solo maneuvers. I listen for Lead's calls in the diamond which gives me a reference for where they are in their maneuver. For an opposing maneuver, like the knife-edge pass, I'll call, "Ninety to the line," to Number 6, which tells him I'm ninety degrees from the show line. We then both nail our airspeeds at 350 knots. We then hack our stopwatches when

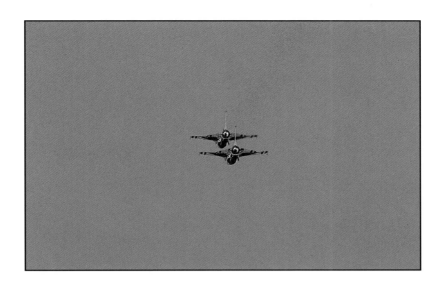

When the solos proceed to join up with the diamond, they will fly a stacked tandem formation, shown above. This solo formation is seen only a couple times during the show. As the solos use afterburner and increase their speed to hasten their rejoin, Number 6 holds position on Number 5 in an extremely pitch sensitive condition. Far more "comfortable" for the solos is their calypso pass, shown below. Note Number 5's floating oxygen hose from the negative G inside the cockpit.

we cross our reference points two miles from show center, and ensure we are at 425 knots groundspeed. It's really nice having the computer read out the winds. At 425 across the ground, it takes us about 30 seconds to fly the length of the show line, so we'll then do whatever it takes to maintain that ground speed. Our window of tolerance is to cross within 150 feet of show center. Beyond that, we know the Logi is going to deduct points from our score, so at the speeds we are flying, we have to be within about one second of our timing. Of course we realize the crowd is just as enthused with a cross that's several hundred feet from show center, but we're not, and we strive to hit it perfectly.

Interestingly, that knife-edge pass, which looks quite tame to the crowd, is actually one of the most violent times in the cockpit for me. Keeping the jet in ninety degrees of bank for the length of the show line is fairly tough, especially if you want to remain level and not turn into or away from the crowd. There is only so much rudder authority on this jet, so I've got to maintain a speed of 500 to 550 to keep enough airflow across that tail for rudder effectiveness. I bring the nose up two degrees above the horizon, then roll left to ninety degrees, push full right rudder, and push to zero G. The G is critical. Anything other than zero and I'll move laterally in relation to the crowd. Basically, it's a maneuver more difficult than it looks.

In today's Thunderbird performance, there are some distinct differences from the solo maneuvers of past teams. Most notably missing are the old "sabre dance" maneuver and the "dirty roll" on takeoff. In the "sabre dance," a solo would slow to landing speeds, lower gear and flaps, and fly down the show line while inducing an exaggerated wing rock, making it appear as if the jet was going to stall out of the sky. In the F-100 days, it was a valid representation of a flight regime more commonly troublesome to jet pilots of that era. With the increased thrust and handling characteristics of the newer jets, the maneuver appeared to be little more than a slow speed pass, and it was replaced with the high AOA pass (Angle of Attack — the acute angle formed between the relative wind and the chord line of the wing). The high AOA pass is a striking demonstration of the F-16's incredible capacity for slow speed flight.

The "dirty roll," a definite nail-biter in the F-4 days, consisted of a solo rolling his aircraft immediately after takeoff with the gear and flaps still down. The F-16, unlike any of its Thunderbird predecessors, represents the "fly-by-wire" technology which incorporates a digital flight control system. Three computers sense, and compare, the pilot's input to the stick, and then send digital commands to the flight controls. With the air refueling door open, or the wheels down, the flight control gains are greatly dampened. The system was designed to preclude a pilot from over-controlling the aircraft during flight phases involving rapid stick movements. With the wheels still down right after takeoff, the roll rate of the computed F-16 would simply be too slow for a safe, low roll.

So just how close do these guys come to each other? In upper photo, the solos have turned hard into each other for a crossing maneuver. The disturbance of lead solo's smoke by Number 6's flight path shows the cross was made a mere few feet behind Number 5's tail. Below, the diamond, at landing speeds, is overtaken by a solo, seemingly threading the formation as he passes close to their side.

Newly added to the solo Thunderbird repertoire, however, is a maneuver that the older jets would never try: the high AOA spiral. Pirouetting high above the crowd, Number 5 holds his jet in a slow speed, high AOA spiral, eerie in its resemblance to a flat spin.

★ ★ ★
★ **5** ★ *It's critical that I enter the spiral at the right speed and angle of attack. By the nature of the high AOA, the dynamics of the maneuver are very different from a normal descending turn. To increase my rate of descent, I would normally push forward on the stick, but now, pushing forward simply reduces the angle of attack, helps the aircraft fly better, and actually slows my rate of descent. If I see I am not descending fast enough, I pull more back pressure, increasing my sink rate with a greater AOA. I have a lot of fun with that maneuver.*

It would be difficult to fly high performance maneuvers in front of large crowds, solo, and not bring some degree of individual style to the performance. Typical of the Thunderbird tradition of professionalism, individualistic inputs on this team manifest themselves in a better overall Team performance, rather than in any individual recognition. In the solo maximum turn maneuver, Number 6 performs a tight 360 degree turn in full afterburner, demonstrating the F-16's incredible turning capability. No one would really notice if the turn were flown at "only" 7 G's instead of 8 G's, but Thunderbird 6 elects to deliver a true maximum performance turn and regularly sees upward of 8.5 G's, a testimony to both man and machine. Additionally, he will fly precisely one degree above the horizon so that the turn looks level to the viewer on the ground.

Also, watch Thunderbird solos performing vertical rolls, and you will see a true vertical flight path, something easily lost when the rolls are done with any G loading. As a technique, Thunderbird solos will pull to a couple degrees past the vertical, then exert a slight push on the stick while rolling "unloaded" vertically, with little or no G on the aircraft to sway its course. Though the crowd is largely unaware of such techniques, they see the results of these efforts in the precision and beauty of a maneuver well flown. Those fighter pilots in the audience who watch every solo's move with a critical eye appreciate such style and know that it separates the accomplished from the merely competent.

As the trail-to-diamond roll is nemesis to the diamond, there is the delta formation for the solos. Bringing their solo routines to exacting levels of skill and timing leaves little time for Numbers 5 and 6 to get really comfortable in the six-ship delta formation. They don't even join the delta until midway through training season, and from then on they retain a deep respect for being on the wing.

Solo Number 6 performs the physically demanding maximum rate turn, above. Below, Number 5 races to join the diamond to form the five-card formation. Guzzling more gas in these types of maneuvers, the solos will normally return from a practice routine ahead of the diamond, due to low fuel. During actual shows, the solos will take off fully fueled, while the diamond aircraft will carry slightly less.

5 *Proficiency on the wing in the delta is a tough one. One of the hardest things we do as solos, is to make that transition from zipping around with our hair on fire, to joining on the delta and maintaining the calm of our wing position. It's like night and day. We fly a deep position in that formation, and that affects us when Lead takes us over the top. He may be pulling a half G in the float, but the next man out is flying a wider arc, so he may be pulling only 0.2 G. I am deeper still, on the end, and usually feel close to zero G. If you look closely, you'll see some different nose positions in that delta over the top.*

After the normal flight debriefing, the solos will usually spend some additional time reviewing tapes from their aircraft's Hud system. These will show them actual parameters flown during certain maneuvers. Also, it will assist them in "helping" the Logi determine if they need to adjust a maneuver to make it look right for the crowd. With a wealth of information, such as speeds, G loading, attitude, angle of attack and time, the Hud camera film is an invaluable aid in helping these pilots to accurately assess each maneuver flown.

6 *One of the most difficult maneuvers for the solos is to split off from the delta and come down to do a series of opposing aileron rolls. First there is the normal "trauma" associated with joining the delta. As we pull up into a delta loop, the full nose down trim always makes it feel like a 6 G pull to me even though Lead is only pulling 4 G's. Just about the time I have settled into the calm of staring at a missile rail, Lead says, "Blue out, ready now," at the top of the loop, and Number 5 and I split off, hopefully in a symmetrical manner. Then in a matter of seconds, we have to immediately orient ourselves to the show line, pick up our reference points, switch the HUD back over to ground speed readout, check the winds, pick up each other, and start making adjustments of one second for every 20 knots of wind correction necessary. In the meantime, we want our noses to arc down at the same rate, so, before we can see each other, we add one G per second in the pull. Once we reach 5 G's, we hold that constant. If Lead splits us off from the delta too soon, we can get some pretty serious ground rush on the way down. A lot is happening quickly and it requires situational awareness, big time. After hanging on through several delta formation maneuvers, I just love to hear Lead say, "Blue out, ready now."*

I know sometimes it looks really dangerous out there, but the way we learn and practice the maneuvers makes it fairly comfortable. I've actually been closer to death in my former squadron, having new guys hurl their aircraft at me during air-to-air practice.

Still, I really get pumped up for each show, because it is the most intense thirty minutes of peacetime flying you'll ever do. During certain parts of the routine, I really have to hustle. I come right off the

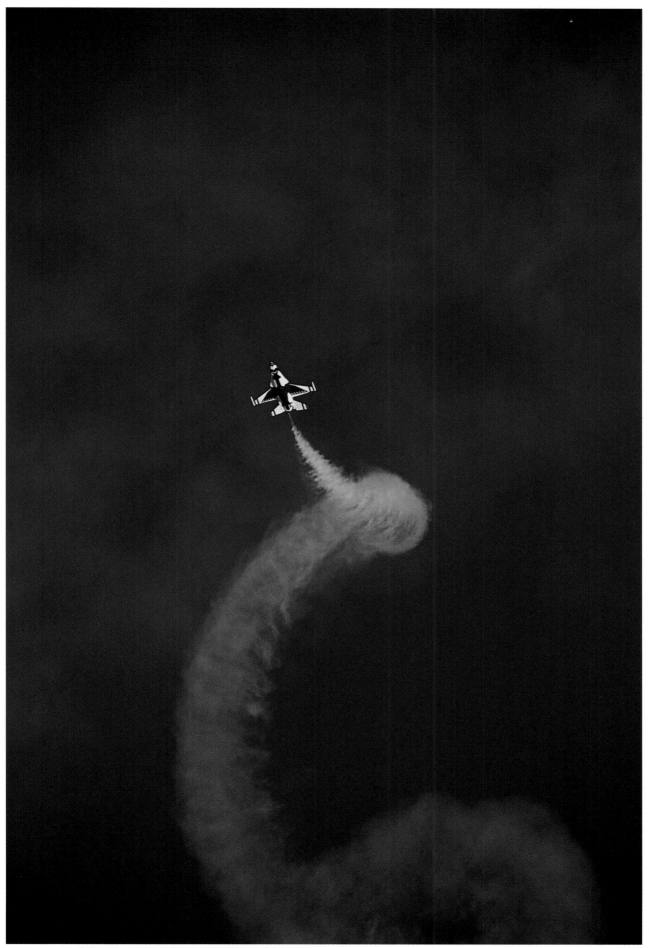

Number 5 performs the Team's newest maneuver, the high AOA spiral descent.

Solo splits off from line-abreast loop and the remaining
four prepare to re-form the diamond.

vertical rolls and then quickly have to reposition from high to low in time to hit that max 360 turn; then, before I can take a breath, right into a half Cuban eight. Some of the hardest maneuvering we do, the crowd never sees as we are repositioning for the next sequence.

I'm a fairly big guy (6 feet 4 inches, 215 pounds) and barely fit into this jet to begin with, so during some of the inverted stuff, I actually have to turn my head a little sideways. I definitely strap in tight and occasionally have had black and blue marks from the straps when I returned. No matter what I do, my legs keep banging the radar switches. Maybe that's why I was having such a hard time with the marching routine. Fighter pilots really don't know how to march. But boy, do we hate to be embarrassed on the video tapes during training. We all march mighty fine now.

5 I feel like any good fighter pilot could be taught to fly these maneuvers. As the lucky one who gets to do it, I try to represent those guys to the best of my ability every time I go out there.

Working together, the solos become very close, and there comes a point where we are thinking in unison out there. When you are hurling your body toward each other at a thousand knots of closure, you really have to feel that trust, and we do. We kid the diamond guys a lot, but we all feel a part of one team.

Don't tell anyone, but I really do think the solos have more fun.

The quiet of the morning desert is pierced with
the sound of a beautifully flown knife-edge pass.

In one of their most challenging roles, the solos "hang on" the left and right ends
of the very beautiful delta formation.

Thunderbird solos live in a world of contrast between the max performance of the individual maneuver and the steadfast constraints of joining the diamond. Here, one solo helps form the five-card formation.

As the delta hits the top of a loop, Lead splits the solos off, and the diamond continues down the back side. The solos can't see this maneuver soon enough.

CHAPTER 5

The Boss

Any formation begins and ends with its leader. It is a critical position, filled only by those with the skills borne of tested experience. In any fighter squadron, the new pilot begins as a wingman and eventually works up to becoming a flight lead. The really good ones seek the position and welcome the challenges and responsibilities which it demands. Though the leader is not actually flying formation on anyone, he can affect the formation quicker and more drastically than any of its members. As the leader goes, so goes the formation, and in the high speed world of flying fighters, there are good things which happen in flight and bad things, and very little room for anything in between.

Thunderbird Lead must be good, very good. All the time, everyday, at every practice and during every show. There can be no mediocrity, no wrong movements and no lapses in judgement. For two years, he will be the single most scrutinized flight leader in the Air Force, by both military and civilian audiences alike. He will set the standard for the Team in everything they will do. Referred to as "Boss" by Team members, Thunderbird Number 1 holds the lives of every man in the formation in his hands, each time he moves stick and throttle. Occupying the single most important position on the Team, the boss sits alone at the front of the formation, flying off no man — leading.

The leader on this team actually wears two hats. He not only leads the formation, but is the squadron commander. Being the squadron commander is probably the more difficult of the two. I now have 140 people that I am responsible for. As Thunderbird Lead, I live in somewhat of a fishbowl and am constantly being watched day in and day out, not only by other Air Force folks and Thunderbird alumni, but by the people in my own squadron. Not only will my flying be the focus of evaluation, but also, how well I lead the squadron as a whole. I know that in the face of some of the turmoil and outside pressures we live with here, I must remain a calm eye of the storm to my people. If I become too agitated over the peripheral stuff, my pilots will sense that and not be in the proper frame of mind I want them in to fly that show.

I'm working with a terrifically talented and enthused group of people, though, and that really makes my job easier. Sometimes they get pretty happy about all they are doing, and I have to reign them in a bit. We definitely stay away from some of the sophomoric activities associated with some fighter squadrons, and the people that come here understand that some things are just not appropriate anymore. I make it a point to greet each new squadron member personally and at that time, I let each person know

Thunderbird Lead sits at the head of the line. On his shoulders rests not only the responsibility for the five men to his right, but the entire squadron as well. Even with all the people the leader will meet in the course of a year, his can be a lonely job.

what I expect from them as Team members. I explain that many doors will be open to them by being on this team, but once they put that Thunderbird patch on, they have given up the ability to act stupid in public and go unnoticed — that door has been closed.

When I look over the applications from pilots wanting to fill flying positions, naturally, they must have the appropriate flying skills necessary, but it's the intangibles which separate the few from the many. We look very hard at a pilot's motivation to be on the Team. It is not an easy process to learn to fly this routine, and fly it well, so we know the desire to really work has to be there. Then of course, we look at how well he relates to people, since we are very much in the business of meeting and talking with people. And, one of the most important questions the Team asks when looking over a pilot's application, is, "how well, as a group, can we live together?" This is important, as we will spend more time with each other during the year, than with our own families. How well we live and work together is important to the Team's success.

Before becoming Team leader, I rode in the back seat in every position to get a good idea of what my guys go through. Once I got out in front of the formation, the hardest thing to get used to was hitting the timing just right. We grade ourselves just as hard on the timing as we do on the maneuvers themselves. Getting that diamond repositioned and back over show center thirty seconds after a solo is quite challenging.

Many times, in repositioning the flight for the next maneuver, show center will be out of sight, directly behind me, and I have to just estimate when to initiate that turn, and how tight to make it, to ensure I'm lined up properly and can hit show center precisely on time. There is no magic formula here; it's just a matter of using basic fighter pilot skills to figure in the winds, adjust the G loading, and eyeball the parameters to make it all work.

Before each show, I will mentally prepare myself the evening before. I study both the aerial photo and the field diagram for that particular show site. In studying the ground references, I try to visualize what they will look like to me from the air and, if the visibility is poor, what other references I might be able to use. I basically "fly" the entire show mentally before actually doing it at the variety of locations we'll see during the year.

In case of poor weather, the Team will fly either a low show or a flat show. The low show will incorporate rolling maneuvers but no "over the top" maneuvers. A flat show will not see either, due to low ceilings, and will incorporate some turns. Each show consists of a radically different set of maneuvers with different timing requirements. The leader must be prepared to transition to each at a moment's notice.

Giving the formation a stable platform to fly off, the Boss leads an arrowhead loop through the vertical. Lead must be consistent in every move he makes.

★ ★ ★
★ **1** ★ *For the Leader, one of the most challenging segments of the whole show occurs during the first*
★ ★ ★ *few minutes of flying. Right after takeoff, the diamond disappears and the solos complete*
★ ★ *their takeoff sequences. Then, two and a half minutes later, we all come across the crowd into*
our opener, a clover-loop. After the solos have split off and we complete the maneuver, I take the diamond
out to reposition for our pass-in-review. In the turn, I will be blind to the show line, my reference points,
and the crowd. I will try to estimate how much wind correction I'll need based on what I quickly saw
on our first pass. I have to plan it precisely, to not only give solo Number 6 time to clear the show line,
but to ensure that I've set the formation for an elliptical ground track-spaced properly from the crowd.
For the pass-in-review, all three aircraft are making adjustments in their position to fly even closer to me
than normal, as we'll arc in front of the crowd in a very tight diamond. This is the most precise formation
we will fly all day, and we have been flying for a grand total of three minutes. How well we fly the pass-
in-review usually sets the tone for how well the rest of the show will go.

When a show really goes well though, it is a great feeling, especially if we are coming off a poor
performance the day before; "poor," of course, being a very relative term here.

The Team leader is aware of the fatigue which can set in during a show season, and watches his pilots carefully to ensure they do not become the least bit complacent flying en route to show sites, as well as in the shows themselves. In this business complacency can kill. Like training season, there can be some long days on the road too.

Occasionally, the Team will be scheduled to arrive at a show site and fly a demonstration that same day, normally a Sunday. That means an early get-up, thorough flight briefing, and a flight to the show site. Once on the ground, all the usual preparations for a show will be accomplished including observation flights, meetings with the air show staff and flight briefing. Following the flying demonstration, there is the autograph session, and any other scheduled public relations activity. Afterwards, the Team will, as always, sit down to debrief the day's performance. They may finally be done by seven or eight o'clock that evening. Just enough time to have a late dinner and sleep before the early flight back to Nellis the next morning. Within twenty-four hours of their arrival home, they will be on their backs, somewhere in the middle of a loop over Indian Springs.

The demands on the pilots from this kind of schedule are the primary reason that a Thunderbird pilot's tour is limited to two years. In past years, pilots served longer, but studies showed that a majority of the Team's accidents involved pilots in their third year. Everyone on the Team agrees that two years is enough, and there are no arguments from their families.

No one, though, feels the pressure of the formation like Lead, literally. As the three jets close in on his plane to form the diamond, he can feel their vortices pushing against his jet to a degree that makes his plane feel a little like an air hockey puck moving across a table. This occurs most

The pass-in-review. It doesn't get any tighter than this.

prominently when he is straight and level and this is one of the few times the diamond can push the Boss around.

★★★★ *I have to be very consistent with the formation, all the time. When I want 4 G's in the pull,*
★**1**★ *I'm not looking for 4.1. The digital readout on the HUD helps and I use it quite a bit. There's*
★★★ *a considerable difference, too, in the onset of the G at 350 knots versus 425 knots, and I have to be careful to adjust my stick movements to keep the boys with me. If I see that I need to change my G by as little as one tenth, I will let them know on the radio and that really helps. Actually, the diamond is quite flexible in hanging in there on some of those repositioning turns when I have had to really tighten it up. I can't maneuver near as aggressively in the delta formation as I can in the diamond, so there's a lot of planning ahead for me in those six-ship maneuvers.*

Normally, with everything else I am watching, I hardly look at the wingmen at all, but I can feel them there. I had the rearview mirrors removed from my jet since I never used them and I'd rather have the better forward visibility. As an old air-to-air guy, if I need to see something behind me, I'll turn and look at it. I took a little heat for that one, though, as I learned that the wingmen had been using my mirrors as a helpful position reference while in the line-abreast loop. The F-16 has such a clean canopy design that there really is very little to use reference-wise.

I don't really feel any added pressure doing a show when there are larger crowds or, say, former Thunderbirds watching. There really is very little time to think about that with all that is happening constantly in the show. That's why we practice just like we are going to fly the show. It enables us to go from one day, flying the routine in front of the Logi at the Springs, to the next day performing the same routine in front of fifty thousand people. Just after taking over the Team, I was given some good advice by Dan Cherry, a former Thunderbird Lead. He said that when people ask about which Team was the best, the answer should always be, "That Team which is currently flying the demonstration, since they are the only ones practiced enough to do it now." "Besides," he said, "you are never going to fly the show as well as former Team members remember flying it themselves."

Each Thunderbird leader brings a certain personality and style to his position which permeates through the entire squadron during his tenure as commander. Each team, over the years, has had its own personality, and each team has been perceived in a variety of ways by both the military and the public at large. Not all of the perceptions have been flattering, or accurate.

When the Team is observed by the public, or even by other Air Force people, during the show season — staying in nice hotels, getting new rental cars (often Ford Thunderbirds), being greeted by dignitaries and catered to at fancy receptions — it is not unusual that some people would think team members to be spoiled or arrogant, receiving all that glittering attention. While realizing that

The Boss leads the delta in front of the show center.

not every Thunderbird was a model person in the Team's forty-year history, Thunderbirds past and present know that the majority of any negative perceptions held toward the Team have been due to a lack of knowledge about how and why the squadron operates the way it does. This is understandable, since so few people, except those who serve, can truly appreciate the hours of continued effort required to produce that thirty minutes of aerial magnificence so many enjoy. That few will truly understand these efforts is accepted by the Team, and will probably never change.

But what has changed, in recent years, is an increased emphasis by Team leaders on giving the Team a more "human" face. The Thunderbirds bring a wonderful message of accomplishment through human endeavor to people all over the world. If those bringing the message are perceived as elite super-humans born with superior skills, then it is a message lost on the many who are inspired by the performance. Thunderbird pilots are simply common people performing the uncommon, in airplanes. They are people who also once came and watched at air shows and who, at one time, thought they could never do this. Standing smartly before the crowd now, they take a joy in revealing, with sincerity, that anyone receiving the type of training they did, could learn to fly like this. Maybe not everyone could, but the statement, delivered honestly, brings the onlooker closer to the pilot, and maybe a step closer to the realization of a dream.

1 *As commander, one of my main objectives is to bring to this team a character which the public will not only appreciate, but be very comfortable with. We don't want to just impress people, we want to relate to them as a hard-working team striving to do our best every day. I think it's great that the public, for a very minimal investment, can come out and talk to some of the folks helping to defend their country. It is wonderful to stand out there and realize that people across this country really do appreciate what we do. Our message of teamwork, discipline and cooperation, can apply to many endeavors besides flying and people tune in to that. We are often asked to speak to groups that have nothing at all to do with flying or the military. I think people enjoy meeting folks who really love their work, and we certainly do. For me, getting to meet and talk with the people is the very best part of my job as Thunderbird lead.*

One thing I definitely stress here is teamwork. I tell all my pilots that we are not out there to showcase individual talents, but to represent, as a team, the talents of the Air Force as a whole. It would be very easy to just go out there and wring out the jet in front of the crowd, and generate individual attention to ourselves, but that is not what this team is about. The precision and professionalism required to perform our show as an integrated team, is certainly more difficult, and is one of the things, I believe, which separates the Thunderbirds from a lot of other teams.

I honestly never thought I would be in this position. It is ironic, though, that my "hero" shot in my pilot training class yearbook shows me posing next to the plane of Thunderbird lead. Like most Air

Twice-a-day flights, after a couple months, can be grueling. The morning sessions did not go well, and the debriefing lasted longer than normal. Unruffled, the Boss is ready for the day's second launch and surveys his "boys" prior to starting. The second flight went better. In fighter squadrons there is no escaping nicknames, not even for the Boss. A close inspection of Lead's gloves reveals the drawing of the likeness of a certain cartoon character.

Lt Col Dan Darnell
Commander/Leader

Force people, I wasn't aware of many details concerning this squadron's history, and when I came here, I was surprised to see that only twenty other men had held the position of Thunderbird lead before me. The responsibility of the position is, at times, enormous, but I have cherished every moment of being commander of such a unique organization.

Though he holds a prestigious position amongst military aviators around the world, Thunderbird Number 1 can, at times, be most humbled close to home. Asked to talk to a third grade class in nearby Las Vegas, the commander stood, waiting in the hallway of the elementary school. He was dressed in a blue, show flight suit, and carried a red helmet to share with the class. Across the hallway stood an eight-year-old boy, staring at the man the way little boys do, with lips slightly parted and eyes looking upward, riveted to the subject. The boy finally spoke.

"Who are you?"

"I'm the Leader of the Thunderbirds."

(Silent blank stare.)

"You know, the jets that fly the air shows right here at Nellis Air Force Base, the white jets you see overhead sometimes — the Thunderbirds."

After a pause and continued stare, "I never heard of you."

At that moment, the Boss was probably thinking that no pass-in-review maneuver was ever this tough.

These are truly men who enjoy what they do and strive each day to do it better. Prior to the start sequence, ramp discussions are common, as everyone wants to find a way to eliminate whatever errors were noted in the last debriefing.

Like other pilots on base, Thunderbirds wear the normal "green bag" to work each day. A practice march-down occurs before every start. It normally takes many to get fighter pilots to march really well. After each flight, there is the debriefing. Lead controls the video and will review the entire flight frame by frame. Afterwards, the solos will spend some extra time reviewing their own aircraft videotapes to validate certain in-flight parameters. The Logi has joined the debrief, on the far left. The mood of these sessions ranges from intense quiet to hearty laughter, but always there is the spirit of cooperative efforts.

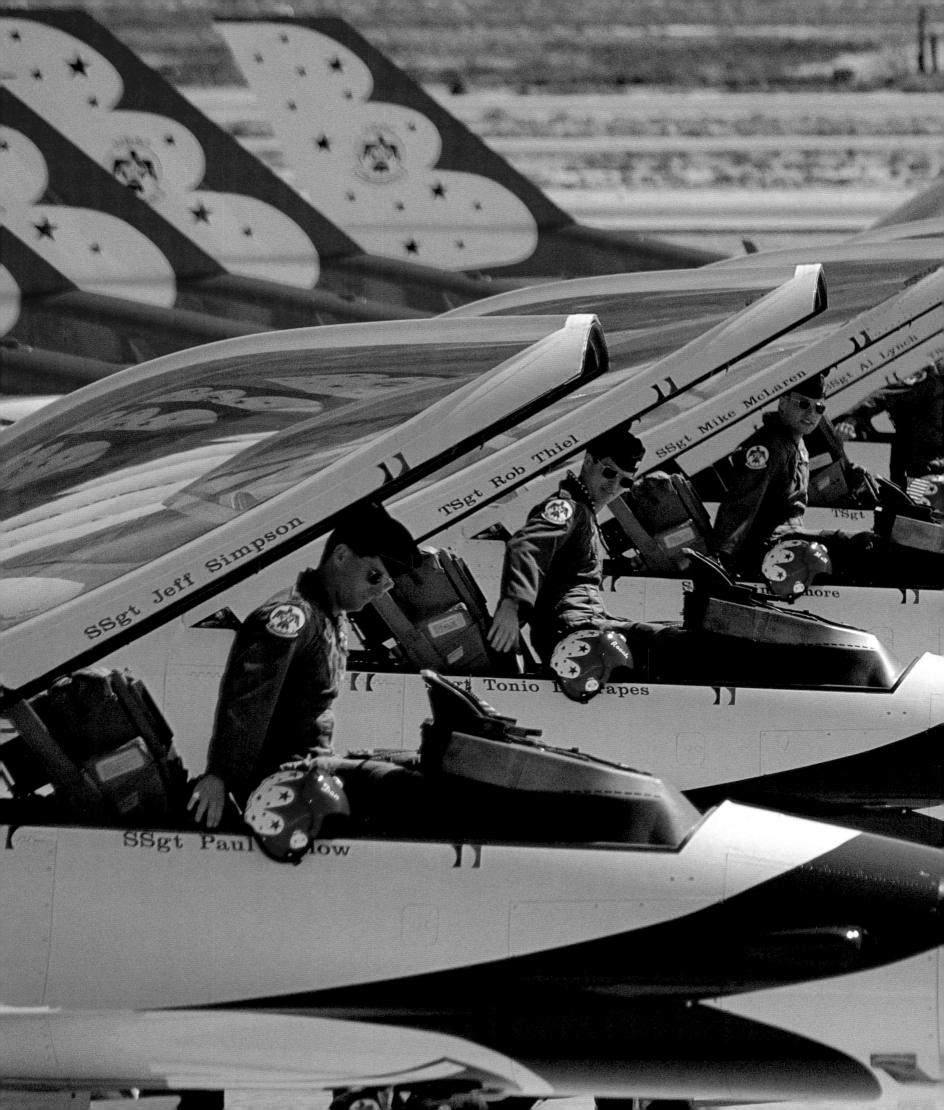

With every practice flight comes a practice start routine.
Each movement is rehearsed to represent a synchronized team.
The F-16 is not a particularly easy jet to enter,
but the team looked good this day.

Thunderbird Lead, somehow, in the midst of training season, has found time to visit a local third grade class. This was not his easiest maneuver. Not only was he not recognized in the hallway, but after he explained for thirty minutes how the Team functions, one student politely asked, "Just what do you do on the team?" Undaunted, Lead pointed out that he was the man in charge, only to receive a barrage of ". . . then why can't you give us a flight?" Showing more patience than most men who fly fighters, the Boss waded through, "How come there are no girl pilots?" and "How do you go to the bathroom in the jet?" He got some help on that last one as his fully outfitted male model responded to his fellow classmate, "That's what the G suit is for, silly." Mercifully, the children's teacher noted at that point that visitation hour was over and the class would have to return to work. Thunderbird Lead was undoubtedly happy to return to the "easy" job of flying fighters.

CHAPTER 6

Plus Two

Besides the six demonstration pilots, there are two additional Thunderbird pilots assigned to the squadron. Though not seen flying in the actual show, Thunderbirds Number 7 and Number 8 are a vital part of every performance. With their help during the training season, the demonstration is made better. Without them during air show season, the show would not go on. They are the logistics officer and the narrator.

On the surface, their Team roles seem easily defined. The logistics officer coordinates necessary aircraft maintenance with flying requirements, and the narrator explains to the air show crowd the maneuvers being flown. In reality, the duties of these two pilots are far more diverse, and valuable, to the squadron.

The Logi actually has to spend only a minimum of time working maintenance problems since Number 11 and his group of "all-stars" on the flight line keep things running quite smoothly. Number 7 is more valuable to the Team as a pilot member who can observe and critique the formation in flight and on the ground. Before the show season ever begins, he'll stand and watch more than one hundred practice demonstrations by the Team at Indian Springs. Besides securing the airspace, and acting as safety observer, the Logi will critically watch every movement of the six demonstration pilots and issue a grade for every day's performance. At the end of the day, he will debrief with the Team back at the squadron.

Number 7 will also fly in chase with the Team sometimes, filming their practices from the air, while Number 8 fills in as ground observer. During the show season, he will fly en route with the other six jets, landing after they have performed any scheduled arrival maneuvers. He will then coordinate all ground activities necessary before any performance. He will serve as the eyes and ears of the six planes in the air during a show, and as such, if he is not in place, equipped with working comm and video capability, the show will not begin.

During training season, the narrator will assist the Logi in flying film chase on the formation while the Logi is observing from the ground. Eventually, once the Team is proficient enough to fly the entire routine, Number 8 will practice his narration at the Springs. The narrator, will, however, spend most of his time coordinating in advance the Team's arrival at the various scheduled show sites.

As the Team's advance man, Number 8 will fly to each show site the day prior to a performance. Flying the two-seater, he will carry with him a maintenance NCO who will ensure that the necessary servicing equipment is available and in place for the Team's arrival. Number 8 will meet with FAA and air show committees to discuss requirements and arrangements for the Team's performance and make note of any airfield peculiarities the Team should know about. Additionally, the Narrator will fly certain media members, or VIPs, in the back seat of his jet in advance of a show.

In the Number 8 position, the narrator flies alone to each show, and often is required to depart a show site prior to the Team. Consequently, he is forced to be separated from the Team frequently and has to adjust to being the Team member the public will most hear, yet least see. In previous years, the narrator would narrate for one year and then move into a demonstration pilot position for the succeeding two years. Today, Number 8 fulfills the position of narrator only, for two years.

THE LOGI

7 *As the chief of maintenance, I will test fly the planes after they have had some major repair work done, prior to releasing them back to the demo pilots. The maintenance officer briefs me daily on the status of the jets and I brief the other pilots on the condition of all the birds. I am basically the guy in the middle of what the pilots want and what maintenance can do.*

Most of my time is spent watching and critiquing the demonstration. It took a while before I was really proficient at doing this. There are so many little things to watch for in the maneuvers. After a while, you start to pick up little movements, or a nose position, that becomes more obvious. The fact that I have not flown in the diamond really doesn't hinder my ability to critique the formation, since I am giving the Team a ground view perspective, something they rarely ever get to see, except on film. And after all, that's where the public is going to view the performance, so I can really help the Team get the right "look" to certain maneuvers.

We basically learn from each other. From numerous debriefings, I have a better idea of what it takes for them to fly their position and they now have a better idea of what it looks like from the ground. Flying the maneuver perfectly doesn't always give the right look to the ground observer, and that's when we get into techniques about how the pilots are going to fly the jet to make it look right. Working out these adjustments to make the maneuver look perfect is a fine art, and that's where I can be a big help to them. When my critiques of their performance are validated on the film, it gives them more confidence in my ability to see the little things. Sometimes they disagree with me, but mostly they know I am trying to make them look better, so there is a feeling of cooperation here. I know my grades to them are important, not only from a self-motivating standpoint, but in that the grade sheets go all the way up the chain to the four-star general level, so I try to be very accurate. Grading the Team "easy" some days, just wouldn't work, since they would see their errors on the film and it would lessen my credibility with them. I try

Demands on the pilot's time are endless. Above, Number 4 comes in on Sunday to draw up the flight plans for the Team's first trip. He will make a copy for each pilot and brief the Team on the route of flight. Below, pilots are joined by the executive and maintenance officers after the day's flying to review the folders of team applicants. An average of fifty to sixty pilots will apply for the Team each year. Only six to eight will be selected to interview in person, and none will know what position they will fly until after selected to the Team. Many times, those selected have applied twice.

to approach my observations like more of a coach, trying to motivate the Team rather than berate their performance.

Even with the videotapes from the ground, my observations, and the in-flight video, these guys are, after all, fighter pilots, and will usually find some way of having some small deviation go undetected. Mostly, though, they are their own worst critics and continually strive for perfection, so we are all working in the same direction.

Flying chase on the Team throughout their maneuvers is a challenge, especially in trying to keep the formation in the HUD camera's field of view. When I first came to the Team, one of the diamond wingmen who was leaving told me that while he would never admit it publicly, flying the proper chase position was probably tougher than flying on the wing. Six jets together, pulling G's, can put out a lot of wake turbulence.

The tough part of learning my job was that I had to spend a great deal of time away from the Team, driving every day out to the Springs to get set up for practices. It gets better during the show season when I am flying along with the Team to each show site. I normally don't join up in close formation with them but fly in chase. I am responsible for keeping them abreast of divert fields along the route of flight in case someone has a problem. If someone did have to land en route, I would go with them, and, if necessary, give them my jet while I stayed with the sick plane. If the plane couldn't be fixed, I'd get a commercial flight to join up with the Team.

One of the interesting things Number 8 and I get to do is fly scheduled media folks in our back seat for promotional purposes. This is either the greatest thrill of their lives, or the worst headache they have ever received. One time we were scheduled to fly this one newspaper writer, who was very cocky before the flight. He made it a point to tell us about how he had flown fighters off of carriers, years ago, and how he really didn't need much of a briefing for the flight. From the amount of weight this man carried, we could only assume that his flying days had ended very long ago. In the course of the flight, actually quite tame by fighter standards, the man screamed, threw up, and passed out. After landing, he sat in the jet for about forty-five minutes before he could stand up. He left in an ambulance.

THE NARRATOR

★ ★ ★
★ **8** ★   *I'm probably on my own more than most Team members. The worst part of that is not getting*
★   ★   *to debrief with the Team very often, as I am already off to the next location. I guess the other*
★ ★ ★   *side of that is when I arrive somewhere, I'm the only Thunderbird in town, and the air show*
folks really do treat me well.

As the advance man for the Team, I try to ensure that their arrival is a smooth process. Sometimes, I'll go into show locations that have never had an F-16 land there before. The two-seater is the heaviest of the jets, so I know if I can land safely, the Team should have no problem with the runway length.

The timing for each maneuver is critical. The Thunderbirds try to have planes in front of the crowd every 30 seconds. As Logi and crew at Indian Springs observe a practice, a record of the timing is kept. The stopwatch shows two seconds remaining for the formation to reach show center in the desired 30 seconds. When not on the ground, the Logi will fly chase to capture aerial video of the formation. HUD camera video is displayed on the cockpit screen in rear seat of 8's jet. On screen is the formation taxiing ahead. Flying behind six other jets can be tricky. While keeping the formation in the camera's view, the chase pilot must ensure his own recoveries and safe separation from the flight during each maneuver. A view is seen of the formation from slightly below the chase position.

I then spend most of my time making sure that all the details necessary for a show have been accomplished. I meet with the air show coordinator to ensure that the show markers are in place, thirty cars are ready for the Team, and the necessary maintenance equipment is available. I work with the FAA representative to ensure that a twelve thousand by three thousand foot show box has been "sterilized." That much space is required so that the jets can reposition during a performance without being a danger to anyone. In that space there can be structures, but no people, during a show. Safety comes first with this team. Sometimes we follow other teams into show sites who have a slightly different approach, and occasionally they have left disgruntled FAA representatives in the wake of their previous year's show. I then have to reassure everyone involved that the Thunderbirds really are going to adhere to specified distances from the crowd and minimum altitudes. My job normally requires a great deal of diplomacy. Most of the time, the air show staff is surprised how flexible we are as a team, and they really enjoy working with us. It's nice when we return to certain locations two consecutive years, because then I've established some rapport with the air show staff and it makes things so much smoother.

As narrator, I spend ninety percent of my time handling the advance work, and only ten percent narrating, but that ten percent is visible to the greatest number of people. As narrator, I have some control over how the crowd feels during a show. My timing is very important and I am constantly monitoring Lead on the radio during the demonstration. I have to be flexible too, in case something unexpected happens. One time the show was halted due to large numbers of birds in the area, and the narrator had to explain to a disappointed crowd what a serious hazard the birds were to jet aircraft. After landing, they found that three of the jets had taken bird strikes. Another time the aft tail cone of one of the solo jets departed the plane and fell into the grass by the runway. I had to reassure the crowd that there was no threat to their safety and then filled the time with a calm assessment of the situation. The solo landed, got into the Logi's jet, took off, and continued the show. There's no script for that sort of thing, so the narrator has to be ready for anything.

Even with all the time I have to spend away from the Team, I really enjoy my position. The opportunity to meet all the people that we do is a wonderful experience. It's great too, being able to fly your crew chief around with you, a situation not often experienced in regular Air Force flying. It's amazing what great service we get when we land somewhere for fuel and pull into the chocks in that red, white and blue jet.

A media member's dream. Thunderbird Number 8 has arrived before
the Team and will take someone up.

Flying a modified chase position, Number 8 maneuvers abeam the formation to critique
the delta en route to the Springs. His comments can help the formation with
spacing on each other, one of the hardest parameters to match.

Those flying with the Thunderbirds should not expect a roomy cockpit. It is a tight fit. Note side-grip stick on right side of cockpit, a radical departure from the standard stick in the center. Every Thunderbird jet is equipped with a stopwatch for accurate timing corrections during the show. The team also displays the stars and stripes in each cockpit.

The narrator will spend much of his time giving incentive flights to squadron members and guests, as shown here with the author.

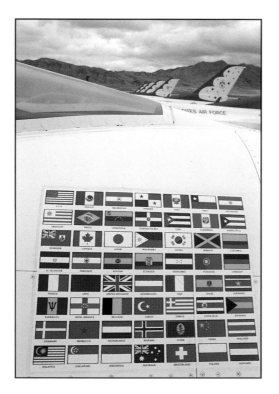

Thunderbird jets proudly display the flags of fifty-six nations they have visited. They also, sometimes, display some flight line humor. Here, the blue "paint" splotch is actually an easily removed rubber sticker strategically placed by a crew chief from another jet. Thunderbird Number 3 watches Lead and 2 intently to match their movements during a practice start sequence.

There will be no splotches.

CHAPTER 7

The Squadron

While millions enjoy Thunderbird demonstrations every summer, the flying they witness is only about one percent of what the Team does on a daily basis. While part of the Team is on the road, a core of Thunderbird personnel remain at Nellis AFB, attending to the various duties required to keep the Air Force's most unique and visible fighter squadron running effectively. Some will never travel with the Team to air shows, but all have a part in helping the Team do what it does best — represent the military to the public.

Officially designated by the Air Force as the Aerial Demonstration Squadron, the Thunderbird organization, though a single squadron, must fulfill the obligations and positions normally associated with a higher air wing level. As a unit, they incorporate their own public affairs office, internally coordinate all team demonstrations, and through their photo and graphics departments, design and secure the printing of each year's new brochures and handouts. While the pilots and support crews are travelling, those back at the squadron continue to run weekly tours of the Thunderbird building, process the folders for new Team applicants, fulfill a myriad of squadron administrative duties, and continue to answer the enormous amount of mail and calls the Thunderbirds receive weekly.

While Thunderbird Number 1 is absent from the squadron, his commander duties are assumed by the executive officer, Number 10. The exec's main function is to run interference for the Boss. He acts as the eyes and ears of the commander in his absence. By serving as somewhat of a buffer, the exec can free the Boss to concentrate primarily on the flying part of his job. This is particularly important during the training season when Lead is flying twice a day, checking out the new pilots. Since Number 1 is gone from the squadron over two hundred days a year, the exec assumes a variety of tasks. He may be doing everything from overseeing the squadron budget, to meeting with the general, to giving a squadron tour to the Girl Scouts. Like many Thunderbirds, he will often arrive for work before the sun rises, and leave for home long after it has set.

NUMBER 10

Occasionally I will make a road trip with the Team, but not often. I actually find myself busier when the Team returns from a trip. Somehow, between the flying and everything else, the pilots manage to do most of their paperwork on the road, and then bring it all home at once for me to process. I am constantly trying to help the pilots in any way I can since they have so little time for themselves. Sometimes the most important thing I can do is make that dental appointment, or call someone's wife to pick up the car, or show one of their buddies around the squadron. The pilots are such regular guys that it really makes my job easier and more enjoyable.

One of the best things this squadron does is to involve its support people in the flying aspect of the mission. Everyone on the Team gets at least one flight in the F-16, and that's a real motivator. More importantly, it helps people get a much better understanding of what the pilots really do. I was in maintenance before coming to the Team, and, like a lot of non-flyers, I joked that pilots were guys that just went out and broke the jets for us to fix. I've gotten three flights with the Team so far, and I have certainly gotten a new perspective on just how hard these guys work. I wish everyone in the Air Force could get that perspective; it's incredible what that does for squadron unity, pride and morale.

My job is never the same any two days. Some days I am meeting with VIPs visiting the squadron, and the next day I'll be stocking the snack bar, or calling for the fitting of the show suits. No matter what, there are never enough hours in the day to do it all. I love working here though, it's a rare opportunity to really make a difference.

My wife and I had a child shortly after coming to the Team, and the squadron made a little blanket for us with the word "Thunderbaby" written across it. You feel the history in this squadron all the time, and you want to do your part to continue that tradition of excellence.

Assisting both Number 1 and the exec, is the commander's secretary. Aside from the two field representatives for the aircraft and aircraft engines, the secretary is the only civilian attached to the Team. Serving the Thunderbirds since 1976, she has seen the face of the Team change many times. She has seen new pilots arrive, and watched them grow during their tour. She has seen some walk out the door to fly who never returned, and she has seen a squadron rebuilt. Throughout it all, she has adapted to working with a new commander every two years.

 Sometimes things can get very stressful around here. There are so many people making demands on the squadron. On any given day people will call for tours, at the last minute an alumnus may want tickets for VIP seating at an air show, someone will be requesting a flight for a magazine article, a group will want the commander for a speech, or some agency on base has a bone to pick with the Team's flight path during the morning practice. The Boss, of course, can't talk to everyone, so I help to refer most of the callers to the appropriate squadron office, normally public affairs.

I never know who is going to be walking up those stairs to our offices. It could be a movie star, a third grade class, or the Secretary of Defense. Having been here longer than anyone, I've seen quite a bit in this squadron and I'd have to say that basically I am prepared for anything, everyday.

I've seen a lot of faces change around here, but the squadron mission and its tradition have remained the same. I tell people new to the squadron that serving the public is our number one priority. In this

Treated with no special favors at its home base, the Thunderbirds are just another squadron on the busy fighter ramp of Nellis. Here an "aggressor" F-16 taxies past the white hangar it sees every day, as Team jets are readied for a practice show.

Solos will normally return from the Springs ahead of the diamond as they are the first to run low on fuel. Note speed brakes opened on rear of jet.

squadron, we treat a young child with the same sense of dignity and importance as we would a four-star general. To be a part of this organization is to serve, and not to expect extra thanks or applause. I see this team away from the show atmosphere, and they work harder than most people realize, and usually harder than they thought they would when selected. The only type of people who should apply here are those with a willing desire to give of their time and of themselves. For those who do, the inner rewards are cherished for a lifetime.

Normally, the squadron members most visible to the public, aside from the demonstration pilots, are those working in Thunderbird public affairs. They serve as the public's main point of contact with the squadron and at least one PA person will accompany the Team on every show trip. Once on the road, they handle media requests, coordinate the necessary protocol at various Team functions, and have to be the "bad guy" who reminds the crews to finish signing autographs with the public in order to meet other commitments. They are also with the Team in case of an aircraft accident, as they would best be able to represent the Team to the media in such an instance.

NUMBER 12

Wearing Number 12, the Thunderbird public affairs officer is assisted by one of the hardest working staffs in the squadron. Constantly in contact with the public, the PA office does not get to switch to a different pace once show season begins. For them, it is a constant effort to try to stay one step, or many steps, ahead of squadron activities, for it is PA who will coordinate it, publicize it, help schedule it, explain it to the pilots, explain it to the public, and then answer for it if anything goes awry. These are people who spend a great deal of time on the phone, and have developed infinite patience in responding to the publics' requests, and demands. They answer that fiftieth complaint of the day concerning jet noise, as pleasantly as the first.

For all their efforts, the PA folks rarely get to see a beginning, middle and end to their projects. Each new day brings new requests, new ideas for next year's brochure, and a deadline for some event months away.

There is no such thing as a standard day here. We are normally working on several projects at once, in between stomping out brush fires. We basically deal with a lot of people who have very little idea what it takes to fly these jets and put this show on, so we try to be very specific in the information we hand out. Most of the media is very good with us, but often we'll see articles full of inaccuracies and we really try to minimize that when possible. We also are quick to squelch rumors that may crop up from time to time. I guess we have a little more pressure on us than most PA offices since

By the end of February, the Team is beginning to look "show-ready." On the runway, final checks are completed by ground crews prior to takeoff. One of the very few things which can halt a Team practice is the weather, and that occurs rarely.

this squadron is very visible to the public and if we say or print something off-key, the whole world is going to let us know about it.

We get some pretty wild requests occasionally. Many people think they can just come out and get a flight with the Team. Others can't understand why the Team can't just come and fly over their hometown.

We receive hundreds of letters each week from people all over the world. The squadron answers every single one of them. We have a basket in the PA office where we stack them, and any squadron member may come in and take some to answer. Even with all the letters we receive, the people here love responding to those who write us, and we never have a problem with the basket getting too full. Sometimes the letters are simply addressed to "Thunderbirds–Nellis" and the post office gets them to us just fine.

Training season is pretty hectic for us since we have to print the new brochures reflecting each year's new faces on the Team. We do that in between writing up the media guides, running weekly tours of the squadron, setting up media flights, and talking with air show coordinators for upcoming events. Life in our office is one continuous interruption. We normally say around here that PA stands for "Practically Anything."

Getting out on the road with the Team is great. In the course of the year, we'll get to meet with some famous people and that's always interesting. This year Arnold Schwarzenegger will be getting a flight in one of our jets. The best part of it all, though, is seeing the faces of those little kids at the shows. That's our greatest reward.

For those of us in the public affairs business, this job is a pinnacle since the Thunderbirds are the showcase of public relations for the Air Force. In order to be effective, we must keep ahead of the schedule by about four air shows. In this squadron, we don't understand the word can't, *we simply* do. *When the Team goes to a show site, we aren't just bringing jets to the public, we are bringing our people, and that's really what it's all about.*

Sitting at a small desk, in an obscure corner of one of the upstairs offices of the Thunderbird hangar, sits the air show coordinator. The sergeant filling this position never travels with the Team to a show, but is the key person in planning in detail, each trip the Team will make during the year. Every aspect of every show, from what the Team will wear to what functions they will attend, will be coordinated in advance.

Cities or bases requesting a Thunderbird demonstration are all given consideration. Once a final list is made, each location will receive a package outlining the support they must provide for the Team, in order to ensure a safe demonstration. Working closely with the operations officer, Number 2, the air show coordinator will take inputs from the pilots concerning certain site conditions which may or may not be suitable for a performance.

Number 2 prepares to strap in for another flight.

Every minute of the pilots' time is accounted for on every trip, and it is the air show coordinator who draws up the itinerary. After 1900, no one is scheduled for anything on a trip, as this ensures pilots have adequate time for rest prior to flying a show.

I'm pretty invisible in the squadron, but that's OK. I don't need to be in the public eye. I know I'm doing a good job when the pilots return happy from their trips. As a team, we try to be fair in selecting which locations will receive a demonstration. Actually, my not going on the road with the Team helps me to be unbiased in my recommendations. Sometimes, sites will cancel on us, and we have no trouble filling the slot. This year we received 905 requests for shows, and we'll be performing at a little over 60 locations. We'd love to do more, but with the cutbacks in the budget we just can't. Occasionally, the Department of Defense will help us decide between locations, since they've stipulated that teams can't return to a site for a third consecutive year if the show falls on a weekend. If that site really wants a demonstration, you'll sometimes see the Air Force performing at Navy bases and vice versa. Also, the DOD insists on deconfliction with the two major flying teams, so you won't see the Air Force and Navy performing at the same location in the same year. These policies are actually good for the public, since they help to bring the teams to the greatest number of different locations in the long run. It's still hard to explain, though, to an air show committee who really wanted to see the Thunderbirds, why we aren't able to meet their request at times.

The most difficult part of my job is trying to find the time to get together with the pilots to brief them on the particulars of their itinerary. They are without a doubt the busiest and hardest working pilots I have ever seen in the Air Force. If they were as egotistical and difficult to work with as some people might think they are, my job wouldn't be much fun. I can't comment on their flying skills, though I assume they are excellent, but I do know that these guys are terrific human beings and a pleasure to work with. I've watched the practice shows here at Nellis a couple times and the flying inspires me every time I see it.

This was not an easy job to learn. There was no checklist or one single way to do it. Now that I'm really good at it, my time on the Team is nearly up. I've loved every minute of it.

The list of squadron support functions is long, and while some squadron members will never go on the road with the Team, their talents and diligent efforts are vital in helping to make that road a little smoother.

It's March, and Public Affairs has scheduled a media day at Nellis. Shortly after landing, Number 4 is interviewed by the local news. "So captain, were you able to see the school kids who formed a human four-zero on the playground in honor of the Team's fortieth anniversary? You flew right over it."

"Well, umm, yes, yes, I believe we did, and it really looked terrific."

(Perhaps when he was inverted in the arrowhead?)

Map of Indian Springs which sits in main briefing room.
Note distance markers to assist with timing. Metropolis
of Indian Springs is seen at bottom.

Air show coordinator's computer screen shows typical pilot's
busy schedule at a show site. Time is GMT.

As evening shadows engulf the ramp, the jets silently await
tomorrow's show, and seem to know that training season
is drawing to a close.

Solos join up with photo-chase on the way home,
high above the Springs.

The last few practices, and the solos are looking very sharp.

The first of two practice shows. Everyone is pumped.

CHAPTER 8

Showtime

There comes a time each year when winter is fading and the first hint of spring arrives with the increasing frequency of blue skies. It coincides with the end of the Thunderbird training season and means that the air show season is fast approaching. Soon the Team will be on the road, publicly demonstrating what they have worked so diligently to create. For the pilots, it is a welcome change from the two-a-day practices they now feel confident to leave behind. They will learn and see a great deal in their travels. As Thunderbirds, they will get a glimpse of America, and the world, that few will ever see. For each pilot, there will be so much more to the experience than can be measured in the movements of stick and throttle they've worked so hard to perfect.

 One of the hardest things on the road, is simply keeping up with your own schedule. With everything else we're doing, it is not uncommon to wake up in the morning and momentarily forget which city you are in.

It is such a wonderful experience, though, to meet different people from around the country. They truly seem to appreciate us being there, and I'm not sure they realize how great that makes us feel. I know the impact we have on the people is far greater than just impressing them with an aerial demonstration, especially when we perform in foreign countries. Last year we performed in Europe, and I remember feeling particularly proud at one airfield, shaking hands with thousands of smiling people. Though I had never been there before, it was a field I was very familiar with. For years it had been on my squadron's primary tactical target list. Had war occurred in Europe, I knew I could have likely been tasked to attack that field. Standing on the ramp of a formerly communist airfield, in front of those red, white and blue jets, was quite a feeling, difficult to put into words. I felt like we were bringing a broader view of not just the Air Force, but America, to these people.

The greatest thing about my job is the positive impact I can have on people. I especially enjoy the young people. When I visit schools, the kids and I often talk about a lot of other things besides flying. So many kids today don't feel they can really succeed the way they would like to and aren't sure they have what it takes. I emphasize to them how important just trying is, and how much difference taking a positive path can make in their lives.

We visited a group of terminally ill kids one time at a children's hospital, and I could see in their faces how much it meant to them that we had come to talk with them. They had the greatest attitudes about life. I felt better about that visit than any four-point roll I ever did.

★ ★ ★
★ **3** ★ *When I am standing out there at a show, I want the people to feel that I am just a regular*
★ ★ *guy who enjoys his job. I want them to be able to relate to me without feeling that I possess*
★ ★ ★ *some special talents they could never have.*
The travel is tough on the family life, but actually I was away from the family more when I was flying the Stealth fighter, so it's all relative. I don't think about the danger of it all — if I did, I would have never been a fighter pilot anyway.

The rewards from travel with the Team are not the pilots' alone, but extend to the many specialists who accompany them on each trip. Since the pilots cannot possibly fill every request for their presence, the enlisted members of the Team will very ably assist in many public relations appearances during the year.

 We get pretty used to people not knowing who we are or exactly what we do out there at the shows. Most folks are very unaware of how many people it takes to keep those jets flying. Sometimes the kids will ask us if we are the pilots and are occasionally disappointed when we tell them no. But then they usually get very interested when we tell them about the variety of other jobs performed on the Team. Talking with the young people at the shows is definitely the most rewarding part of this job. I know we have had a positive influence on some of these kids, you can just see it in their faces.

Before departing Nellis each year, the Thunderbirds will kick off the air show season with a show for the people of Indian Springs, flown at that field, and a second demonstration flown at Nellis. Besides providing a final close scrutiny by notable alumni and the base generals, the Nellis demonstration offers the families of Team members an opportunity to enjoy their very own show. Officially marking the end to the training season, the kickoff show points the Team toward the long road of summer air shows ahead.

During the show season, they will spend four to five months away from home. Ninety percent of all the flying hours they log will be spent traversing the distances between show sites. And when they do return home, they will be exhausted, but will, of course, spend more time refining the formation at the Springs.

The crew chiefs are the most visible enlisted members of the squadron during a show. They take an intense pride in their jet and get to know their pilot well.

Number 5 roars down the runway moments after takeoff. Note gear door still open.
Crowd response at shows is always intriguing.

Solos make the cross at the Springs, and the boys have a good one going
in front of their first crowd of the year.

The enormous physical and emotional drain on the pilots throughout the year validate the wisdom of a two-year tour length. The wives and families of team members endure the tour at home, with the kind of supportive camaraderie normally found in most fighter squadrons. Children of squadron members are referred to as "Thunderkids," and squadron events throughout the year are planned to bring them together. Occasionally the wives will meet their husbands at show sites close to Las Vegas. Far from the past images of bachelor fighter pilots on tour, Thunderbird pilots today are nearly all married, with two to three children, and view their families as the main priority in their lives.

Once on the road, the Team will represent many things to many people. For some, it will be the first time they have seen military jets, or ever talked with an Air Force pilot. The responsibilities and challenges of being in the public's eye can be as demanding for the pilots as learning to fly the formation. As one pilot put it, though, "Once I could move smoothly from trail to diamond, I figured I could do anything."

And so it goes on; for over forty years now, each spring a new formation of Thunderbirds has taken flight and touched the hearts and minds of millions of people everywhere. Though the technology has changed, the display of precision formation which exemplifies the Thunderbirds is as exacting and difficult as it was with that first straight-winged diamond formation. Today, the jets fly faster and turn tighter, but the Team's important message of pride and professionalism remains unchanged. In the process of demonstrating the strength and capabilities of today's Air Force, they make Americans, both military and civilian, feel good about their service and their country. During show seasons when the Team travels overseas, they often will perform to audiences watching their first F-16s, as well as meeting their first Americans. On many occasions, likely more than are realized, Thunderbirds have truly served as America's "Ambassadors in Blue."

The message of teamwork, discipline and pride which the Thunderbirds bring to audiences each year, is introduced boldly at each show by the team jets, but transmitted most poignantly by the men and women who are the Team. To meet and talk with Team members is to revel in the positive, feel a certain motivation toward excellence, and gain an awareness of the possibilities of fulfilling one's own dreams. Though much has changed over the years, that Thunderbird spirit, like the formation, has steadfastly remained.

Each show season will be unique. No two Teams will bring the same faces to the public, as people in the squadron will change each season. Each year's Thunderbird formation will carry its own distinctive signature, even while flying the same maneuvers of previous teams. Occasionally, show maneuvers will change, such as the addition of the high spiral and removal of the "dirty roll" with the F-16. This is rare, however, and many Thunderbird maneuvers, carefully chosen to represent various skills and capabilities, have remained the same over the years. New Thunderbird pilots frequently bring fresh ideas and requests for new maneuvers, but like many of their Air Force

The Nellis show must satisfy the generals but, more importantly, must pass the scrutiny of that man in the middle, Retired General W.L. Creech, former TAC commander, and former Thunderbird. He is invited each year to the kick-off show. The team never looked better than on this day. Even the Logi's scores were up.

A rare view of the bomburst from above.

It's not practice, and it's not Indian Springs, but the Logi still watches — and comments.

It's showtime.

"Really, I'm serious now — the solos do have more fun."

counterparts, face a bureaucratic obstacle course in order to secure higher approval for the change. Even so, changes do occur, which improve the demonstration. A recent example is the repositioning of the trail-to-diamond roll entry angle, giving the crowd a better view of the dynamics of the formation's movements.

While both dangerous and difficult, the Thunderbird demonstration will most often be called, simply, *beautiful*, by the many who will witness it each summer. It is a beauty hard earned by those few creating it, and they cherish the opportunity to share it. Team pilots accept that few may understand the subtle intricacies of all they have labored to perfect, but that is all right. They simply want people to enjoy the show, however they view it.

Those performing and those watching the performance will have radically differing views of the show, and in the diversity that is an air show crowd, some on the ground will be oblivious to the intensity of effort occurring above them.

But the Team will know, as they will not only fly the demonstration, but will feel it as well. In every turbulent bounce encountered, with each flirtation with fear, from every sunlit reflection causing sweat-soaked eyes to squint, in every flexed right forearm, and with every heart-stopping near miss, they will know the show as few can, and feel it. And in those few minutes they will taste life at its fullest. It is the silent and sweet reward for those who know what it is to climb every step of the mountain to its peak. And in the midst of it all, the Team will note every minor deviation. It is the price required when striving for perfection.

When that show opener is dead solid perfect and the boys have a good one going, performer and audience become one in their celebration of the performance. Somewhere in the middle of the five-card loop, Number 3 will see all his references on Lead's jet motionless and he'll know, for the moment, that he is rock solid in his position, and the aviators in the crowd below will marvel at the perfect symmetry of the five airplanes. Two solos will pass each other at show center, on time to the second, and the kids in the front row, caring little about the time, will press their hands to their ears and shriek with delight. Somewhere, someone in the crowd will flinch, then laugh in surprise, as Number 5 screams across their head in full 'burner on the "sneak pass." In just a few quick moments in front of the crowd, four jets will move with apparent ease, from trail into diamond, and no one will hear the "whoa" likely vocalized in at least one of the cockpits. And in the final minutes of the demonstration, the boss will take the delta across the top of a loop, easing six jets earthward in a powerfully smooth arc, and someone in the crowd, staring silently skyward, will feel a lump in their throat, and an inspiration which, if they knew, would make the men in the loop smile.

At show's end, the pilots, sweat soaked and exhausted, will climb down from their jets and once again touch an earth wonderfully solid under foot. They will enthusiastically sign their names for thousands of eager people, and will enjoy their moment in the sun, as they have earned it.

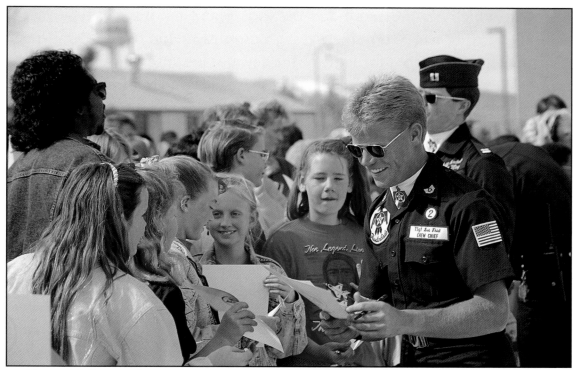

Crew chiefs may sign as many autographs as the pilots at a show. Here, school kids at Indian Springs get a morning free from class.

Number 3 attends his first autograph signing. He was as excited as the kids in the crowd.

Number 2 gets a hug from his top fan — Mrs. Number 2.

In a world in which we are reminded daily of man's failures, witness the Thunderbird demonstration and simply feel good about the accomplishments of successful people working together as a team. They don't do it for fame or money, but because they choose to strive to be the best at what they love doing. Simple in concept, it becomes powerful in its presentation.

For reasons they find difficult to describe, some people are moved to tears while watching a Thunderbird demonstration. Perhaps it is because they realize that more than just speed and sound, the proper execution of the rigid demands of formation flying can reveal a delicate beauty that all can savor. All that is required is for one to look upward.

S AIR FORCE
UNITED STATES AIR FORCE
USAF
UNITED STATES AIR FORCE

Somewhere during the show season, some young person will watch the formation, and become mesmerized, and rush to see the jet, once parked. And a life will be altered.

In Appreciation

Since the emphasis of this book is on the Thunderbird experience, and not one specific Team, I intentionally avoided the use of individuals' names throughout the text. Were it not for the cooperative efforts of one specific, and special Team, however, this book could not have been completed. The members of the 1993 Thunderbirds were not only gracious hosts, but exceptionally worthy representatives for the concept of this book. I expected excellence, and they exceeded that expectation.

I observed this Team in flight and on the ground, at both work and play, in the squadron and off duty, in their homes. Already quite familiar with Thunderbird operations, I knew I would not be easily impressed during my stay with the squadron. This Team impressed me in a variety of ways and gave credence to my initial desire to write this book. In all this Team showed me, I was left with the impression that I could have observed the squadron during any year and would simply have pictures of different people carrying on the same standards of excellence. Celebrating their Team's fortieth anniversary, I felt these remarkable people deserved mention in a book they were so integrally a part of. With deep respect and appreciation, I have included on the following pages the names and positions of the men and women of the 1993 Thunderbirds.

Additionally, I have included a picture of the pilots since, without them, there would be no book. Instead of the official public relations photo that is so often seen of these men, I wanted one less formal, depicting them more as they actually were on a daily basis. In reviewing my slides, I was not surprised to see that most showed these men smiling, for they truly love what they do. I saw one that best represented to me a fitting close to this book. On the morning this Team would leave Nellis for their first official show of the season, I asked the pilots, resplendent in their show suits, to get together for a quick picture before they took off. I had specifically not asked them to pose for any pictures during my stay, and humorously watched as members of one of the world's most photographed organizations appeared slightly awkward, revealing a basic camera shyness. Theirs was the most human of responses and represented much of what I admired most about this team. This photograph, taken moments before they would climb into the jets, captures the Team pausing, ever so briefly, on the bridge which links the training season to the beginning of a new show season. The genuinely happy faces of these men say more about all they have accomplished than I could ever write. I had the pleasure of knowing them as individuals, and the privilege of observing them coming together as a team. Fighter pilots everywhere can be proud they are being represented by men of such high caliber.

My month spent with this group of talented and enthused people was an enlightening and refreshing experience I will cherish forever. Throughout it all, I was repeatedly reminded of the joy I first felt watching their predecessors many summers ago. Long may they continue to fly.

(Left to right) — "Dagwood," lead; "Roach," left wing; "Birdman," right wing; "Kuda," slot; "Buck," lead solo; "Abner," opposing solo; and "Boots," logistics officer. Typically , the narrator had already departed for the show site. Pictured separately is "J.K." in whom I had great trust as he flew me for all the shots taken from chase.

The "Boys"— fighter pilots all — Thunderbirds

Thunderbirds 40th Anniversary Team

LtCol Dan Darnell-Commander\Leader

Capt Jeff Rochelle-Left Wing

Capt Matt Byrd-Right Wing

Capt James Evanko-Slot

Capt Clark Rogers-Lead Solo

Capt Peter McCaffrey-Opposing Solo

Maj Michael Major-Logistics Officer

Capt John Switzer-Narrator

Capt Paul Reagan-Executive Officer

Capt Walter Sarafin-Maintenance Officer

Capt Eric Schnaible-Public Affairs Officer

CMSgt Keith Deberry-Maintenance Superintendent

SMSgt Mike Jarnegan-First Sergeant

SMSgt Mike Devine-Public Affairs Superintendent

SMSgt Gary McCue-Quality Assurance

MSgt Doug Bieber-Flight Chief

MSgt Al Hall-Production Superintendent

MSgt Joseph Hudson-Line Chief

MSgt Jay Jennings-Inspection Flight Chief

MSgt Joyce Langston-Airshow Coordinator

MSgt Rex McIntyre-Specialist Flight Chief

MSgt James Moats-Maintenance Operations Flight Chief

MSgt Dave Ramey-Resource Advisor

TSgt Jim Baker-Aircraft Maintenance

TSgt Rusty Bennett-Crew Chief #8

TSgt Mark Blackburn-Crew Chief #1

TSgt Pat Boylan-Electrical Systems

TSgt Gordon Fenley-Engines

TSgt Joel Fulmer-Structural Maintenance

TSgt Donna Garland-Structural Maintenance

TSgt Ron Givens-Training

TSgt Dave Hunnewell-Aerospace Ground Equipment

TSgt Kelly Kibbey-Weapons

TSgt Ron Jackson-Aircraft Maintenance

TSgt Mark King-Aircraft Maintenance

TSgt M. Martinezjunco-NCOIC, Information Management

TSgt Ron Mihalko-Egress

TSgt Dwayne Pate-Fuel Systems

TSgt Mark Payne-Aircrat Maintenance

TSgt Dan Phillips-Logistics Coordinator

TSgt Larry Reese-Aircraft Maintenance

TSgt Bill Rountree-Egress

TSgt Emilio Sandoval-Supply

TSgt Jose Santos-Crew Chief #8

TSgt Sandy Stacey-Avionics

TSgt Robert Thiel-Crew Chief #2

TSgt Gary Thompson-Crew Chief #7

TSgt Malcom Turner-Environmental Systems

TSgt Roger Uptegraft-Weapons

SSgt Keith Allen-Crew Chief #7

SSgt Larry Alfonso-Aircraft Maintenance

SSgt Bradley Appleby-Engines

SSgt Sal Belloise-Aircraft Maintenance

SSgt Philip Benjamin-Life Support

SSgt Mike Cavanaugh-Video

SSgt Jeanette Clukey-Personel

SSgt Coy Coward-Communications

SSgt Tony Cox-Information Management

SSgt Mark DuLac-Weapons

SSgt Cecil Ennett-Information Management

SSgt James Farley-Avionics

SSgt Gerald Fore-Aircraft Maintenance

SSgt Dean Fritz-Aircraft Maintenance

SSgt Timothy Grunst-Aircraft Maintenance

SSgt Dale Harris-Supply

SSgt Robert Hoyle-Information Management

SSgt Linda Ipser-Public Affairs

SSgt John Kelly-Pneudraulics

SSgt Bill King-Illustrator

SSgt Greg Kimoto-Crew Chief #6

SSgt Tonio Lastrapes-Aircraft Maintenance

SSgt Tim Leath-Aircraft Maintenance

SSgt Mike Lightner-Life Support

SSgt Dave Liliedahl-Communications

SSgt Bill Lisowski-Crew Chief #5

SSgt Alfred Lynch-Crew Chief #4

SSgt Deborah Lyons-Aircraft Maintenance

SSgt Daniel Mattioda-Electrical Systems

SSgt Mark McGowan-Plans and Scheduling

SSgt Don McKim-Airborne Video

SSgt Michael McLaren-Crew Chief #3

SSgt Albert McPherson-Aircraft Maintenance

SSgt Mike Moore-Photographer

SSgt Lincoln Nealy-Operations

SSgt Jim Palmer-Aircraft Maintenance

SSgt Tim Patterson-Structural Maintenance

SSgt Paul Pellow-Stuctural Maintenance

SSgt Tony Pettaway-Avionics

SSgt James Pomeisl-Fuel System

SSgt Dale Posey-Aerospace Ground Equipment

SSgt Sherman Powell-Aircraft Maintenance

SSgt Roberto Rodriguez-Aircraft Maintenance

SSgt Anthony Sabatine-Aircraft Maintenance

SSgt Mike Schuller-Video

SSgt Jeff Simpson-Crew Chief #7

SSgt Richard Street-Aircraft Maintenance

SSgt Bryan Walker-Structural Maintenance

SSgt Mary Whitehouse-Plans and Scheduling

SSgt Elliott Williams-Avionics

SSgt Ron Young-Information Management

SSgt Bill Zink-Aerospace Ground Equipment

Sgt Wendy Ayers-Supply

Sgt John Berlan-Aircraft Maintenance

Sgt Darren Herrera-Personnel

Sgt Bobby Hunt-N.D.I.

Sgt Matthew McKinney- N.D.I.

Sgt Tracy Seganos-Maintenance Analysis

Sgt Yuk Tam-Maintenance Analysis

Sgt Manuel Valderez-Supply

Sgt Chris Winston-Aircraft Maintenance

Sgt Jeff Wolfe-Photographer

Sgt Brian Yenke-Information Management

SrA Frank Boyd-Fuel Systems

SrA Kevin Elmore-Environmental Systems

SrA Ernesto Franco-Fuel Systems

SrA Tim Guy-Avionics

SrA Todd Isaacson-Aerospace Ground Equipment

SrA Melodie Lagasca-Information Management

SrA Rodney Leblanc-Pneudraulics

SrA Cecile Martinez-Operations

SrA John Melito-Egress

SrA Tony Murphy-Avionics

SrA Chris Rash-Electrical Systems

SrA Scott Stoeckle-Communications

SrA Carol Weller-Environmental Systems

SrA Shawn Yoder-Structural Maintenance

SrA Jason Young-Fuel Systems

Mr. Jeff Brookshire-Lockheed Rep

Mr. Juergen Odlum-Pratt & Whitney Rep

Ms. Maureen Walker-Commander's Secretary

UNITED STATES AIR FORCE

Photo Notes

Over 5,000 transparencies applied for a position as demonstration pictures in this book. After a difficult and demanding selection process, only 140 were used in the formation of this story.

The Springs sit desolately quiet now, in the midst of air show season. Soon the skies will be filled with the penetrating sounds of Thunderbirds overhead, beginning anew the process of building a formation. For now, the summer sky brings only the sound of distant thunder.

Autographs